Sweetie Pie's Cookbook

Sweetie Pie's
COOKBOOK

SOULFUL SOUTHERN RECIPES,
FROM MY FAMILY TO YOURS

ROBBIE "MISS ROBBIE" MONTGOMERY

WITH **RAMIN GANESHRAM**

PHOTOGRAPHY BY CHRISTOPHER HAWKINS
AND LEYNA NOELANI AMBRON

Amistad
An Imprint of HarperCollinsPublishers

SWEETIE PIE'S COOKBOOK. Copyright © 2015 by Robbie Montgomery and Timothy Norman. Photographs copyright © by Christopher Hawkins and Leyna Noelani Ambron. All rights reserved. Printed in the United States of America. No part of this book may be used or reproduced in any manner whatsoever without written permission except in the case of brief quotations embodied in critical articles and reviews. For information, address HarperCollins Publishers, 195 Broadway, New York, NY 10007.

HarperCollins books may be purchased for educational, business, or sales promotional use. For information, please e-mail the Special Markets Department at SPsales@harpercollins.com.

FIRST EDITION

Designed by Suet Yee Chong

Library of Congress Cataloging-in-Publication Data has been applied for.

ISBN: 978-0-06-232280-7

15 16 17 18 19   ov/QGT   10 9 8 7 6 5 4 3 2 1

FOR MY MOM AND POP, WHO WERE EXCELLENT COOKS
WITH AMAZING PALATES. FOR MY SISTERS AND BROTHERS,
WHO ATE UP EVERY DAMN THING OUR PARENTS PREPARED.
WISH WE WERE ALL STILL TOGETHER.

CONTENTS

INTRODUCTION

When I was sixteen years old and helping my mother cook dinner for my eight brothers and sisters, the last thing I was thinking about was a cookbook. Where I'm from folks didn't cook out of cookbooks, much less write them—you just cooked! Someone taught you and you taught someone else. That's how it was in my family.

Now my family has gotten too big to teach each and every one of you my secrets in person—that's right, I said *you*. All you folks who come into Sweetie Pie's and watch *Welcome to Sweetie Pie's* on the Oprah Winfrey Network and all you folks who have listened to my music all these years are part of my family. *Sweetie Pie's Cookbook* is my opportunity to share my special recipes with you, just like you were standing next to me in my own kitchen.

As far as I'm concerned, the most important thing to know about how I cook is that this is food with *soul*. That means you put your heart into it, you put your love into it, and you put your history into it. Soul food is more than just a style of cooking that has come out of the African American experience; it's the true melody of *American* food. As long as I can remember, we have taken whatever we've had and made it sing—no matter how poor or few those ingredients were. Our food—soul food—tells a story about survival.

In addition to sharing some amazing recipes, I will share my own story of survival. Every dish has come out of my real life experiences—whether it was

Miss Robbie and her sisters Linda and Janice, in the lobby of the original Sweetie Pie's Restaurant, in Dellwood, Missouri.

learned from my mama, my friends, or while I was on the road. Sometimes those experiences were sweet and sometimes they sure could be bitter, but all of them have made me who I am. And through it all, no matter what, I was always cooking.

Over these many years, I've learned to listen to my own gut and my own taste buds when I cook. I love to experiment, and I love flavor with a capital *F*—that's why you're going to notice that when a teaspoon of vanilla or a dash of a spice will do, I up the ante and add as much as I think will make the flavor pop! Now I understand my heavy hand won't appeal to everyone, so I encourage you to be your own kind of experimenter. That's the best way to make these dishes your own—from my kitchen to yours.

Nowadays when people go out to eat or when they open a cookbook they're looking for appetizers or starters or whatever you want to call them. As long as I've known soul food I've never known anyone to talk about "courses" or the idea that the meal should be divided up in some way. In fact, dessert is just about the only serving that was thought of as separate from the rest of the meal.

Since I do know that it's much more handy to have a book divided up into courses, that's what you'll see here. You'll also see tips on making some of these recipes lighter. We all know that soul food is heavy on ingredients like butter and other fats and sugar and salt, and while these enhancers are tasty (who can deny that?!), we know that we have to be a little more careful about how liberal we are with these ingredients.

My personal philosophy is moderation: I may eat a tiny sliver of pie, but I want the real thing, no substitutes. That's why you'll see that the suggestions I make for cutting down on sugar, fat, and salt are still high in flavor—otherwise, what's the point?

I've even come up with my own recipes for ingredients that many people have come to depend on to add flavor to their food, including powdered onion soup mix and canned celery soup, or even, believe it or not, Velveeta-style cheese!

You may wonder why I went ahead and reinvented the wheel. "Why not leave well enough alone, Miss Robbie?" The reason is simple: health and quality. Do you know what all goes into making packaged food? I sure don't. But I *do* know what goes on in my own kitchen, and I know that I can do a lot better creating these recipes myself.

With that housekeeping aside, I want to say that most of all I hope you enjoy this book, and that you make all of the recipes and share them generously with your family and friends so we can keep soul food alive and thriving.

And while I know this book is going to turn you into a mighty fine soul food cook, I hope you won't forget to stop in and see me at Sweetie Pie's.

Robbie Montgomery

OPENING ACTS

salads, soups, and nibbles

When we'd put out the spread at the family table, whether it was for everyday or a special occasion, the best thing you could have was a full spread, and that meant that deviled eggs were bumping up against fried chicken or that a soup was being slurped down even while someone else was making a grab for some macaroni and cheese. I realize that folks eat differently now and sometimes we just want to fix up something light or we want to make a meal out of a lot of little dishes for a party. What you'll find in this chapter are just those types of dishes—everything from soup to salads and small bites that can serve as snacks or appetizers.

HOLE IN ONE

When I worked as a kidney dialysis technician, one of my favorite patients was Mr. Leon Strauss, who loved my cooking enough to lend me the money to open the first Sweetie Pie's. I'd often bring him soul food favorites; in exchange, he taught me about the hole in one, a fried egg inside of a piece of skillet-toasted bread, which many people might recognize as "Texas Toast." It's a quickie meal that I like to make for breakfast, but you'll love it for brunch or lunch as well. I generally keep it simple; to make it a little fancier, I'll add some minced chives or shredded cheese. A side of bacon or sausage is a perfect companion.

SERVES 2

2 slices Texas Toast
2 tablespoons butter, softened
2 large eggs
Salt and pepper
1 teaspoon minced fresh
  chives (optional)
1 teaspoon minced onion
  (optional)
2 teaspoons shredded cheddar
  or other cheese (optional)

1. Heat a large skillet over medium heat.

2. Cut a round about 3 inches from the center of each slice of bread.

3. Butter both sides of the bread and lay them down on the skillet. Fry for 1 minute, then crack an egg into the hole in each slice. Cook the egg until it's just set, about 1 minute, then sprinkle with salt and pepper.

4. Flip each slice of bread and fry for 1 to 2 minutes more depending how firm you like your eggs.

5. If you want to add chives, onions, or cheese, gently break each yolk before flipping and sprinkle the ingredients evenly onto the yolks, then flip the bread and cook as directed in step 4.

ONION SOUP

Onion soup is a reliably warming dish on a cold day. My recipe lends itself to improvisation—you can add vegetables, little meatballs, or egg noodles and make a whole new soup out of it. If you're not finishing your soup with croutons and cheese, serve the bowls with Roberta's Grandmother's Yeast Rolls (page 128).

SERVES 4

1 tablespoon unsalted butter

1 large sweet onion, such as Vidalia, thinly sliced

3 cloves garlic, thinly sliced

5 cups beef broth

1 bay leaf

Salt and pepper

1 cup large croutons (optional)

1 cup shredded mozzarella cheese (optional, if adding croutons)

1. Melt the butter in a large saucepan over medium-low heat and add the onions. Cook low and slow, stirring often, until the onions get nice and brown but don't burn, about 5 to 6 minutes.

2. Add the garlic and cook for a minute or two, until it just starts to brown.

3. Add the beef broth and bay leaf and season with salt and pepper. Raise the heat to high, then reduce the heat and simmer for 15 to 20 minutes, until the soup is reduced by about a quarter.

4. Spoon into bowls and serve with yeast rolls if you like. Or, if you're using the croutons and cheese, preheat the broiler. Divide the soup among four ovenproof crocks, distribute the croutons among the crocks, and sprinkle with the cheese. Put the crocks on a cookie sheet and place under the broiler until the cheese is browned and bubbly, 1 to 2 minutes. Serve immediately.

miss robbie says . . . back it up! Onion soup makes a great flavoring for other dishes, like my Oniony Roasted Corn (page 102). Try freezing the soup in ice cube trays; dump the soup cubes into a zip-top freezer bag or a resealable container so you can take out a few cubes at a time to add to stews, gravy, or other dishes calling for a little stock.

CREAM OF CELERY SOUP

Canned cream of celery soup was one of those items my mom always had on hand to add flavor to a stew or a smothered chicken recipe. I make my celery soup from scratch. It's delicious on its own, and it can make other recipes like my Baked Chicken and Rice (page 32) and Chicken and Dumplings (page 33) sing.

SERVES 4 TO 6

1 tablespoon unsalted butter

1 small onion, minced

2 cups minced celery

1 tablespoon all-purpose flour

6 cups hot chicken broth

1 teaspoon salt

1 teaspoon ground white
   pepper

1 sprig fresh thyme

1. Melt the butter in a large saucepan over medium heat. Add the onion and celery and cook until the celery is softened, about 10 minutes. Add the flour and cook, stirring, for 1 to 2 minutes, until lightly colored but not browned.

2. Stir in the hot broth until the flour is incorporated, then add the salt, pepper, and thyme. Bring to a simmer, then lower the heat to medium-low and simmer for 15 to 20 minutes.

3. Serve as the opening course of a Sunday Roast Beef (page 74), or separate into individual containers and freeze to use as an ingredient in other recipes.

HOMINY STEW

Growing up, we ate our share of stew because it was cheap to make yet filling; a little could go a long way to feed many people. This stew is a classic soul food recipe that uses two ingredients most dear to any southerner's heart: hogs and corn. Hominy is dried split corn kernels; folks could store hominy all winter long and add to any long-cooking soup or stew to make it thick and hearty.

The stew goes well with Roberta's Grandmother's Yeast Rolls (page 128) or Hot Water Cornbread (page 121) served alongside.

SERVES 6 TO 8

1 cup dried hominy or
  1 16-ounce can hominy,
  drained and rinsed
1 tablespoon vegetable oil
1 small onion, minced
2 cloves garlic, minced
1 pound smoked ham hocks
  or smoked turkey
1 bay leaf
3 sprigs fresh thyme
1 cup stewed tomatoes
1 teaspoon ground black
  pepper

1. If using dried hominy, soak it overnight in a bowl covered with 3 cups of water, then drain.

2. Heat the oil in a soup pot over medium-low heat. Add the onion and cook just until it starts to soften, then add the garlic and cook for 1 or 2 minutes more, until it just starts to brown.

3. Add the ham hocks and 6 cups water. Toss in the bay leaf, thyme, stewed tomatoes, and pepper. Raise the heat, bring to a simmer, then reduce the heat to medium-low and simmer for about 1 ½ hours, until the ham hocks are good and tender.

4. Remove the ham hocks from the pot and place on a cutting board. Cut the meat from the bones into bite-size pieces. Return the meat to the pot and discard the fat and bones. Simmer the stew for another 20 minutes to blend the flavors and serve.

my terrific trio Onions, green bell peppers, and my homemade onion soup mix (page 183) are included in about 90 percent of what I cook. It's the flavor combination that makes these classic soul food recipes my own. Because I'm an experimenter, I always encourage folks to go ahead and try things their own way. You may prefer red or yellow or orange peppers, or maybe even a little fresh hot pepper. Any way you mix it up, Sweetie Pie's Terrific Trio keeps folks coming back for more.

OXTAIL SOUP/STEW

Oxtail was expensive when I was growing up. When my mom made oxtail soup, she'd only use one or two oxtails when we could have easily done with five or six for a family our size. She'd fill out the soup with beans or potatoes and vegetables; enriched by the delicious broth made from the oxtails, it tasted amazing. I cook my oxtails a good long time to make sure the meat falls off the bone. Roasting your oxtails in the oven first will give the soup a nice rich color and taste; it will also give you some nice drippings to mix back into the soup for flavor but you can also make the soup by simply adding the oxtails to the pot with the water, onion, and onion soup. The vegetable I like to load up on is corn, but you can use any combination that tastes good to you.

Serve with Roberta's Grandmother's Yeast Rolls (page 128), Hot Water Cornbread (page 121), or crackers.

SERVES 6 TO 8

3 pounds oxtails

Salt and pepper

1 cup tomato sauce

1 tablespoon sugar

6 tablespoons onion soup mix, homemade (page 183) or store-bought

1 medium onion, chopped

2 large Yukon gold potatoes, peeled and cut into cubes

2 carrots, chopped

2 cups fresh corn kernels or frozen niblets

2 cups fresh okra, stemmed and cut into 1-inch chunks

1. Preheat the oven to 400°F.

2. Season the oxtails well with salt and pepper and put them in a baking dish. Bake until browned, about 1 hour, and remove them from the oven.

3. Pour 2 tablespoons of the oxtail drippings into a bowl and add the tomato sauce and sugar. Mix well and set aside.

4. Put the oxtails in a large soup pot along with 8 cups of water, the onion soup mix, and the onion. Bring to a boil, then reduce the heat and simmer, skimming foam from the top of the pot as needed, for about 1 hour, then add the tomato sauce mixture. Cook for another hour, or until the meat starts to easily pull away from the bone.

5. Add the potatoes and carrots and simmer for 15 to 20 minutes, until the vegetables are fork tender. Add the corn and okra and simmer for about 10 more minutes, until softened, and serve.

miss robbie says . . . do a punch-in In place of the oxtail, you can make this recipe with boneless beef short ribs cut into 1-inch pieces. Follow the directions above, adding about 1 tablespoon vegetable oil to the beef when you roast it, as it won't have as much fat as the oxtail. Reduce the total cooking time by about 30 minutes, until it's nice and tender, and you've got yourself a beef stew.

CRAB DIP

I serve crab dip at parties. To me it's like dressed-up tuna salad, or, as I like to say, "black folks' caviar." You can serve crab salad inside scooped-out tomato halves, or with crackers, slices of French bread, or sliced tomatoes, or in lettuce cups as a party dip. For my crab dip, I pick the meat out of whole crabs, but you can certainly use canned crab. Chopped cooked shelled shrimp also makes a good substitute.

SERVES 6 TO 8

1 pound fresh crabmeat,
  picked and shredded
⅓ cup mayonnaise
1 small onion, finely minced
1 small green bell pepper,
  cored, seeded, and finely
  minced
Salt and pepper
1 hard-boiled egg, minced

Mix the crabmeat, mayonnaise, onion, and green pepper together in a medium bowl. Season with salt and pepper. Gently fold in the hard-boiled egg, taste, and adjust the seasoning. Serve as suggested above.

DEVILED EGGS

Deviled eggs, a satisfying side dish, are great for barbecues and picnics, but we like to make them anytime there is a big gathering. They are easy to make and are put together with ingredients that are usually on hand: eggs, sandwich spread or mayonnaise, mustard, and a little salt and pepper. Sometimes I add a little cut-up shrimp, chicken liver, or crispy bacon to the mix, and I like to sprinkle a little cilantro on top just before serving; you could also use parsley or another herb you like best.

MAKES 12

6 hard-boiled eggs

3 tablespoons sandwich
   spread or mayonnaise

1 tablespoon prepared
   mustard

½ teaspoon sugar

Salt and pepper

¼ cup minced sautéed chicken
   livers, ¼ cup minced cooked
   shrimp, or ¼ cup finely
   crumbled crispy bacon
   (optional)

Paprika for garnish

Minced fresh cilantro for
   garnish

1. Slice the eggs lengthwise and gently scoop the yolks out into a medium bowl. Mash the yolks well with a fork.

2. Add the sandwich spread, mustard, and sugar and mix well. Season with salt and pepper. Stir in the chicken livers, shrimp, or bacon, if using.

3. Using a teaspoon, spoon the yolk mixture back into the egg white halves. Arrange on a platter and sprinkle with paprika and cilantro, if using.

SALMON CROQUETTES

I like to serve salmon cakes with grits for breakfast, or better yet, sandwiched between a homemade Baking Powder Biscuit (page 127) all hot and buttered up. You'll take one bite and feel like you're knocking at heaven's door.

SERVES 4

1 (15-ounce) can pink salmon, drained, juice reserved

1 small onion, minced

1 small green bell pepper, cored, seeded, and minced

1 large egg

½ teaspoon salt

½ teaspoon ground black pepper

¼ teaspoon cayenne pepper (optional)

10 to 12 saltine crackers, crushed into crumbs

3 tablespoons vegetable oil

1. Place the salmon in a bowl and flake it apart with a fork. Add the onion, bell pepper, and egg, then mix in the salt, black pepper, and cayenne pepper, if using.

2. Add the saltine crumbs a little at a time until you can form the mixture into a small meatball and it holds its shape. If the mixture becomes too dry, use some of the reserved salmon liquid to moisten it. Discard any unused liquid.

3. Form the salmon mixture into rounds the size of golf balls and flatten them into small patties. Place them on a tray and refrigerate for 15 minutes.

4. Heat a large skillet over medium heat and add the oil. Heat for 1 to 2 minutes, until nice and hot, then gently place the salmon patties in the skillet, taking care not to crowd them. Fry for 4 to 5 minutes, until lightly browned, then gently turn them over and fry on the other side for 4 to 5 minutes more, until lightly browned on the second side. Serve immediately.

POTATO SALAD

I'm a stickler about potato salad. In our family, my sister Linda is the best potato salad maker, and she's the one who makes it when we get together. Potato salad is the invited guest at every party, and it even goes with our barbecues, Thanksgiving, and Christmas meals. There are a couple of secrets to this recipe: the first is mashing the potatoes slightly so you don't have a lot of big chunks in the salad; the other is using sandwich spread, a mix of mayonnaise and sweet relish that's popular in the South. The absolute must-have ingredient is finely chopped hard-boiled eggs—enough to taste but not enough to overpower the mix.

SERVES 4

4 large Yukon gold potatoes

1 tablespoon plus 1 teaspoon salt

6 hard-boiled eggs

1 stalk celery, minced

1 small green bell pepper, cored, seeded, and minced

½ medium onion, finely chopped

½ teaspoon ground black pepper

¼ teaspoon celery salt

1 teaspoon sugar

2 tablespoons sour cream

6 tablespoons sandwich spread

6 tablespoons mayonnaise

1 tablespoon yellow mustard

1 tablespoon pickle relish (optional)

Paprika for garnish

1. Fill a large saucepan with water and add 1 tablespoon of the salt. Add the potatoes and bring to a boil over medium-high heat. Reduce the heat and simmer for 25 to 30 minutes, until fork tender. Remove from heat, drain, and cool until they are easily handled.

2. Peel the potatoes, cut them into 1-inch chunks, and place them in a large bowl.

3. Finely chop 5 of the hard-boiled eggs—you want them about the size of half your pinky fingernail—and set aside. Slice the remaining egg into thin rounds and set aside.

4. Add the celery, bell pepper, onion, the remaining 1 teaspoon salt, the pepper, celery salt, and sugar to the bowl and mix well. Using a potato masher, gently mash the potatoes so they are broken into smaller pieces but not mashed smooth.

5. Add the sour cream, sandwich spread, mayonnaise, mustard, and pickle relish, if using. Add the finely chopped eggs and mix very well. Spoon the potato salad into a salad bowl or casserole dish, arrange the egg slices on top, and sprinkle with paprika.

6. Cover and refrigerate until ready to serve.

a little sweetie pie's love
You are going to find that many of my recipes call for a little sugar, also known as "a little Sweetie Pie's love." It's usually just a dash, not to make the food taste sweet but to enhance the flavor, the same way salt does. I learned this trick from my mom and from a lady called Miss Johnson who worked at a snack shop in St. Louis called Billy Birk's.

CHICKEN SALAD

When we were growing up, my cousins didn't like pieces of onion in their food, so my aunt came up with a way to get the flavor of the onions in her chicken salad without the kids knowing about it: she pureed the onions and mixed them into the chicken salad along with the mayonnaise or sandwich spread, and now it's something we all do. I prefer to eat chicken salad on butter crackers or saltines, but of course it makes a great sandwich filling too; I also like it stuffed inside a scooped-out tomato half.

SERVES 4

1 pound boneless chicken
   breasts
2 cups chicken stock
¼ teaspoon salt
¼ teaspoon ground black
   pepper
½ small onion, processed
   to a rough puree in a food
   processor
1 stalk celery, trimmed and
   roughly chopped, then
   processed to a rough puree
   in a food processor
1 small green bell pepper,
   cored, seeded, and roughly
   chopped, then processed
   to a rough puree in a food
   processor
6 tablespoons sandwich
   spread
2 tablespoons mayonnaise
Paprika for garnish

1. Place the chicken breasts in a medium saucepan. Add the chicken stock, salt, and pepper, place over medium heat, and bring to a simmer. Reduce the heat and simmer until the chicken breasts are cooked through but still tender, about 30 minutes.

2. Remove the chicken breasts from the pan and shred the chicken with a fork or cut into small pieces. Reserve the leftover chicken cooking liquid for soup, if desired.

3. Place the chicken in a medium bowl and add the onion, celery, bell pepper, sandwich spread, and mayonnaise. Taste and adjust the seasonings as needed. Sprinkle with paprika and serve on crackers or bread.

COLESLAW

Coleslaw is one of those dishes that goes with just about everything. It's a must-have at a barbe-cue or picnic, pairs perfectly with chitterlings (page 52), and goes especially well with fried fish. Because it's such a versatile side dish, every family makes it and boasts their own spin. Some folks use sour cream (I don't). Others will use a little lemon juice, but I prefer vinegar, which helps soften the cabbage without it getting mushy. The most important thing is that it should be creamy but not so creamy that all you taste is the dressing, and the cabbage should be slightly softened with just the right amount of crunch. After traveling all over the country and tasting a whole lot of coleslaw, this is the version I'm proud to call my own.

MAKES 6 TO 8 SERVINGS

1 small or ½ large green
   cabbage, cored and finely
   shredded
1 small or ½ large red cabbage,
   cored and finely shredded
1 small sweet onion, such as
   Vidalia, finely shredded
1 carrot, finely shredded
½ green bell pepper, cored,
   seeded, and finely shredded
½ cup white vinegar
1 tablespoon raisins
1 cup milk
2 cups mayonnaise
2 teaspoon salt
1 teaspoon ground black
   pepper
¼ cup sugar

1. In a large bowl, combine the green and red cabbage, the onion, carrot, and bell pepper. Add the vinegar and mix very well, then add the raisins.

2. In a separate bowl, whisk together the milk, mayonnaise, salt, pepper, and sugar. Pour the mixture over the cabbage mixture and mix well. Cover with plastic wrap and refrigerate overnight before serving.

SOULFUL TACOS

The first time I ever had a taco was when I was on the road with Ike and Tina. We were headed west, to California, and had stopped in Arizona to play some gigs. We sat down in a Mexican restaurant—the first one I'd ever been to—and I ordered the tacos because I had heard people talking about them. When those tacos came to the table, I didn't want to act like I didn't know what I was doing, but I didn't. I took my fork and scraped everything out and ate it that way. It wasn't until later, when I lived in Los Angeles, did I learn the right way to eat a taco. I came to really like the mixture of meat, cheese, lettuce, and tomato folded over into a tortilla, but I figured I could do it one better with a little soul food styling. The result was my Soulful Taco, which is grilled in a skillet to make the taco shell lightly crispy and the cheese inside nice and gooey. I use either ground beef or steak for my tacos, but you could use chicken, shrimp, or even grilled vegetables if you like.

GROUND BEEF OR TURKEY TACOS

MAKES 4 TACOS

½ pound 80% lean ground beef or ½ pound ground turkey

1 small onion, minced

1 small green bell pepper, cored, seeded, and finely chopped

1 (1.5-ounce) packet taco seasoning mix

8 medium corn tortillas

½ cup shredded Colby cheese

½ cup shredded Monterey Jack cheese

1 cup shredded iceberg lettuce

1 small tomato, chopped

4 tablespoons prepared salsa

1. Heat a large skillet over medium heat and add the ground beef. Cook, stirring to break it up, until the beef is cooked through and browned, about 15 minutes. (If you are using ground turkey, heat about 1 teaspoon of oil in the skillet before you add the turkey, and it will only take 6 or 7 minutes for it to brown.) Stir in the onion and bell pepper and cook for another 5 minutes, or until the onion and green pepper soften.

2. Stir in the taco seasoning mix and cook for 1 minute. Remove the meat mixture from the pan with a slotted spoon. If you are using ground beef, drain off most of the fat (ground turkey will not have much fat left). Place a corn tortilla in the skillet and fry it until it's crisp, about 30 seconds, then turn over and crisp up the other side. Remove it from the pan and place on a plate. Repeat with a second tortilla.

3. Combine the two cheeses. Spoon a quarter of the meat mixture onto the tortilla in the pan and add ¼ cup of the shredded lettuce, a few pieces of tomato, 1 tablespoon of the salsa, and ¼ cup of the cheese. Place the second fried taco on top and gently turn it over to brown the other side for about 30 seconds, until the cheese melts. Repeat with the remaining tortillas and filling to make 4 tacos. Fold it up like a taco and lay on the plate. Serve immediately.

STEAK TACOS

MAKES 4 TACOS

2 teaspoons vegetable oil
½ pound New York strip steak
Salt and pepper
1 small onion, cut into slivers
1 small green bell pepper, cored, seeded, and cut into slivers
1 (1.5-ounce) packet taco seasoning mix
8 medium corn tortillas
½ cup shredded Colby cheese
½ cup shredded Monterey Jack cheese
1 cup shredded iceberg lettuce
1 small tomato, chopped
4 tablespoons prepared salsa

1. Heat a large skillet over medium heat and add 1 teaspoon of the oil. Season the steak with salt and pepper on both sides and place it in the skillet. Cook the steak for 3 to 4 minutes on each side for medium rare, 6 to 7 minutes for medium, and 8 minutes on each side for well done. Remove the steak from the pan to a cutting board and cut it into small pieces. Set aside.

2. Heat the remaining 1 teaspoon oil in the pan, stir in the onion and bell pepper, and cook for 5 minutes, or until the onions and green pepper soften.

3. Return the steak pieces to the pan, stir in the taco seasoning mix, and cook for 1 minute. Remove the steak mixture from the pan with a slotted spoon and drain off most of the oil. Place a corn tortilla in the skillet and fry it until it's crisp, about 30 seconds, then turn it over and crisp up the other side. Remove it from the pan and place on a plate. Repeat with a second tortilla.

4. Combine the two cheeses. Spoon a quarter of the meat mixture onto the tortilla in the skillet and add ¼ cup of the shredded lettuce, a few pieces of tomato, 1 tablespoon of the salsa, and ¼ cup of the cheese. Place the second fried taco on top and gently turn it over to brown the other side for about 30 seconds, until the cheese melts. Repeat with the remaining tortillas and filling to make 4 tacos. Serve immediately.

Thirty years ago, I packed my bags, took my young son, and headed back to St. Louis from Los Angeles, a city I called home for nearly twenty years. Up until then I had been a working singer, first in my own bands and then, later, as a backup singer for artists including Bonnie Raitt, Rita Coolidge, Glen Campbell, the Rolling Stones, and many more. As far as making it as an entertainer went, I had been pretty lucky. In a lot of ways, I was living a dream.

But then my luck ran out.

I was diagnosed with an illness that collapsed my lungs, left me with sarcoidosis, and ended my singing career. Suddenly I found myself without a job and no way to support young Tim and me.

Singing was the only job I had ever had from the time I was twenty years old. I didn't know how to do anything else—or so I thought.

That was when all the things I learned in my mama's kitchen and cooking on the road finally paid off: I realized I could cook for a living, so that's what I set out to do. For a short time, I had a little wings restaurant in Pomona, down below Los Angeles. I got folks into the place with my "try before you buy" policy: I gave them a single wing, and if they liked what they tasted they'd come in for more.

For a short time, I made it work, but then one too many bouts of bad luck including break-ins where everything in the place was stolen, plus being in a city where I didn't have any folks or friends started to get to me. Eventually, I packed up for good and went back to St. Louis.

When I got there things weren't much easier. My family didn't have much more than I did, so I knew I couldn't lean on them too hard. I also knew the restaurant business took money, so I gave up on that too. I bit the bullet and went to school to be a kidney dialysis technician. The money was steady, I got good at it, and I was comfortable, but there was always something nagging at me. I wanted to do my own thing.

In that time, I had developed a friendship with one of my patients, Leon Strauss, a St. Louis developer, and his wife, Mary. I'd cook

Miss Robbie and her son, Tim, in front of Sweetie Pie's Restaurant at the Mangrove location in St. Louis, Missouri.

for them, sharing my soul food recipes. I told Mr. Strauss I wanted to open a restaurant; he didn't discourage me like most everyone else had.

Mr. Strauss also told me he didn't want to back a restaurant because most restaurants fail. He was right about that. Instead, what he and Mrs. Strauss did was give me a little here and there to buy equipment or rent a place. They'd tell me to ask for what I needed, and I never asked for too much—a couple of thousand maybe—because I didn't really know how much things cost, and I also had my pride. They knew, though, and they never said no.

The first place we got was an old bakery. It was fully outfitted, so I thought I was on my way. Boy, was I wrong. The hood wasn't the right one for a restaurant and the health department wouldn't give us our licenses. All of a sudden, this great place turned out to be a dog, so I went and sold all of my music equipment for $20,000—a lot less than it was worth—to buy what I needed. Then I sold the car I had just bought for Tim, who needed it to get to work.

After all of that, I couldn't afford to pay for anything else. The restaurant was put together with tables, chairs, and dishes that I bought at garage sales or got from other people. I quit my dialysis job, even though everyone thought I was crazy. The restaurant was my last chance, so I got my nerve up and did what I had to do. Now that I had a skill as a technician, I could go back

to it if had to, but I prayed that I wouldn't have to.

There was no staff at that first location in Delwood, just me and family friends Miss Betty and Miss Annie. Together we cooked, cleaned, washed dishes, and served customers.

The business was slowly becoming profitable, but Mr. Strauss died before I was really making the restaurant work. When one door closed another opened. I met another kind man who believed in me—Mr. O'Brien. He helped me buy my first condominium in the Florissant section of St. Louis by giving me the mortgage himself. When a place with a restaurant on the bottom and a dentist's office opened up in the neighborhood, he took me to his bank and got them to give me a loan when no one would take a risk on me.

Those first few years were hard, but we kept on going. The day that I came to work and I saw a line at the door before we even opened was the day that I knew we could be successful. But I never take anything for granted—it's a tough business that's one part luck and ninety-nine parts sweat, labor, and prayer. Even now, after thirty years, a slow day gets me nervous.

That was the very first Sweetie Pie's, and it's still open today. Now there are four Sweetie Pie's, three in St. Louis and one in Memphis. Who knows, there may be another Sweetie Pie's in another city sometime soon.

HOT HONEY CHICKEN WINGS

After I left St. Louis for my singing career and later returned home, I found that hot chicken wings had become really popular. Most versions were too spicy for my liking, so I started experimenting with recipes, adding honey and butter to cut down on the heat, and that's how my hot honey chicken wings were born. You can go beyond wings and use the glaze with any fried chicken recipe.

SERVES 4 TO 6

FRIED CHICKEN WINGS

3 pounds chicken wings (drumettes and
    wings)
2 cup all-purpose flour
2 teaspoons salt
2 teaspoons ground black pepper
1½ teaspoons paprika
4 teaspoons garlic powder
2 large eggs
1 cup buttermilk

1 to 2 cups vegetable oil for frying,
    enough to fill the skillet halfway

HOT HONEY GLAZE

³/₄ cup (1½ sticks) unsalted butter
1 cup hot sauce of your choice, or to taste
2 cups sugar
¼ cup honey
1 teaspoon lemon juice
3 tablespoons soy sauce

1. Rinse the chicken under cold running water and pat dry.
2. In medium bowl, whisk together the flour, salt, pepper, paprika, and garlic powder.
3. In a separate bowl, beat the eggs, then beat in the buttermilk.
4. Dip the chicken wings into the egg-buttermilk mixture, then place them into the seasoned flour and toss them to coat. Remove the wings from the flour, shaking off any excess, and place them on a baking sheet. Refrigerate for 15 to 20 minutes.
5. Heat the oil in a large skillet over medium heat until a thermometer registers 350°F or a pinch of flour dropped into the oil immediately sizzles and fries hard.
6. Add the wings and fry for 5 to 10 minutes on each side, until the juices run clear when a wing is pricked with a fork.
7. While the chicken wings are frying, make the hot honey glaze: Melt the butter in a medium saucepan over medium heat. Add the hot sauce, sugar, honey, lemon juice, and soy sauce and stir until the sugar is dissolved and the mixture begins to thicken.
8. Remove the chicken wings from the pan and toss them in the glaze. Serve immediately.

miss robbie says . . . put it on rewind! To lighten up this recipe, you can bake the chicken wings instead of frying them. Season the wings with your salt, black pepper, paprika, and garlic powder. Lightly spray an ovenproof baking dish with cooking spray and spread the wings out on the dish. Bake the wings at 400°F for 25 to 30 minutes, until they are cooked through, then toss them in the hot honey sauce. Serve with a salad or fresh-cut french fries seasoned with salt and pepper.

MAIN MELODY

fish & seafood, poultry, pork & beef

When I think of the main part of a soul food meal, I think about a good hearty dish that can fill you up and leave you satisfied. Usually that will be the meaty part of the menu—fried chicken, smothered pork chops, a roast, or a juicy hamburger.

In this section of the book, you'll find seafood, poultry, and meat dishes that serve as the main event, with everything else on the table circulating around them. I've written my recipes to generally serve the standard four to six—much smaller portions than we offer at Sweetie Pie's or that we made at home with nine of us in the house.

In traditional soul food cooking you'd use what you had, or what you could get, and you made it work. Back in the day, this meant a lot of wild meat and cured meat that had to last through a winter. Today we can get anything we want at the supermarket—and for a lot less money than folks in other parts of the world pay for their food—but that doesn't mean we should forget how to use a variety of cuts of meat in the best possible way. This philosophy is reflected in the recipes in this chapter. After all, I work hard, and my ingredients should too.

CATFISH FILLETS

Filleted fish is a good option for those who don't want to pick around the bones of a whole fish. It is also the most easily found variety of catfish—available in most grocery stores. Serve this version of my fried fish with Potato Salad (page 14), Coleslaw (page 17), rice, or a green salad.

SERVES 4

2 pounds catfish fillets
Salt and pepper
1 cup cornmeal
¼ cup all-purpose flour
1 large egg
1 cup vegetable oil

1. Wash the catfish fillets under cold running water and pat them dry. Season with salt and pepper.

2. In a large bowl, whisk together the cornmeal and flour. In a separate shallow bowl, beat the eggs well. Dip the fish in the beaten egg, then dredge it in the cornmeal to totally coat it.

3. Heat the oil in a large, deep skillet over medium heat until a pinch of flour dropped into the oil sizzles. Lay the catfish into the oil and fry until golden brown, 5 to 6 minutes per side. Remove from the pan and serve.

FRIED WHOLE CATFISH OR JACK SALMON

Growing up, we always ate fish on Fridays. Even though my dad and his friends would go fishing, we'd mostly get our fish from the market. When my dad did get lucky, he'd mostly reel in crappies, little fish that we'd cook whole. Buffalo fish, a bony river fish, was a favorite, what the adults would eat because of all the sharp bones, and thin-boned whiting for the kids. Whiting, also known as jack salmon, can be found frozen in the fish market, and it's popular in restaurants served fried whole or in fillets, just like catfish. What I've given you here is a classic fish breading, but at Sweetie Pie's we have our own special mix—look for it your grocery store real soon!

Serve with Potato Salad (page 14), Coleslaw (page 17), rice, spaghetti, or a green salad.

SERVES 6 TO 8

1 (5- to 7-pound) catfish or
   jack salmon, head removed,
   gutted and scaled
Salt and pepper
1 cup medium grind yellow
   cornmeal
¼ cup all-purpose flour
2 large eggs, well beaten
2 cups vegetable oil

1. Wash the fish very well under cold running water, particularly in the cavity area to make sure there are no innards remaining. Pat the fish dry and season with salt and pepper inside and out.

2. In a large shallow bowl, whisk together the cornmeal and flour. In a separate shallow bowl, beat the eggs well. Dip the fish in the beaten egg, then dredge it in the cornmeal to totally coat it.

3. Heat the oil in a large, deep skillet or Dutch oven over medium heat until a pinch of flour dropped into the oil sizzles. Lay the fish into the hot oil and fry until golden brown, 12 to 15 minutes for catfish and 10 to 12 minutes for jack salmon. Serve immediately.

EVERYTHING BUT THE KITCHEN SINK GUMBO

When you get set to make gumbo, plan on making a big pot, because it's a dish that's meant to serve a crowd. Gumbo comes from Louisiana, but here I've made it my own by adding my favorite ingredients. While you'll find old-school Cajun ingredients like gumbo filé powder, roux, andouille sausage, and shrimp in my gumbo, I also include crab, lobster, and a whole chicken.

When I make this gumbo, my friends and family come over with two bowls—one to eat from and another to take home. I happen to like to eat my gumbo with saltine crackers, but the traditional way is to spoon it over plain white rice.

SERVES 10 TO 12

1 (2-pound) whole chicken

1 large yellow onion, finely chopped

2 green bell peppers, cored, seeded, and finely chopped

2 stalks celery, finely chopped

4 tablespoons (½ stick) unsalted butter

⅓ cup all-purpose flour

½ pound andouille sausage, sliced into 1-inch rounds

1 tablespoon gumbo filé powder, or more to taste

1 cup chopped okra

2 pounds snow crab legs or stone crab claws

2 pounds lobster tail

1 pound shelled and deveined large shrimp

1 tablespoon hot sauce, or to taste

Salt

1. In an 8-quart stockpot, combine the chicken, onion, bell peppers, and celery. Add 6 quarts of water, place over medium-high heat, and bring to a soft boil. Reduce the heat and continue to simmer for 20 to 30 minutes before adding the roux, skimming the top as needed.

2. Meanwhile, make the roux: Melt the butter in a medium skillet over medium heat. Add the flour and cook, stirring constantly, until you have a light brown roux, 2 to 3 minutes. Add the roux to the pot with the chicken and stir well.

3. Heat another medium skillet over medium heat, add the sausage, and cook until browned, turning it once, 7 to 8 minutes. Remove the sausage pieces with a slotted spoon and add them to the chicken mixture.

4. Continue to cook until the chicken is tender enough to pull easily from the bone, about 1 hour. Remove the chicken from the pot, cool slightly, and pull the meat from the bones. Discard the bones and skin and return the chicken to the pot. Add the gumbo filé powder and simmer for 10 minutes, or until the filé begins to thicken the gumbo.

5. Add the okra and simmer for 10 to 12 minutes, then add the crab and lobster tail and simmer for 5 to 7 minutes more. Add the shrimp and cook until just pink, about 2 minutes.

6. Stir in the hot sauce and season with salt. Serve over rice.

BAKED CHICKEN AND RICE

This is another one of my mama's easy one-potters, a dish she often made in the summer. While it's cooking it leaves you time to do something else. Be sure to wash the rice well so it doesn't get sticky. To wash rice, put it in a bowl and add twice as much cold water, swirl it around with your hand, then carefully pour off the cloudy water, taking care not to pour out the rice with it. Do this a few times until the water is mostly clear, then drain the rice in a colander and set it aside to add to the chicken as it's baking.

SERVES 4 TO 6

1 (3-pound) chicken

1 teaspoon salt

1 teaspoon ground black pepper

3 teaspoons No-Salt Seasoning Mix (page 182)

1 tablespoon all-purpose flour

4 cups Cream of Celery Soup (page 5)

2 cups water

1 medium onion, chopped

2 stalks celery, trimmed and chopped

4 tablespoons (½ stick) unsalted butter, cut in half

1 cup white rice, washed

1. Preheat the oven to 375°F.

2. Rinse the chicken inside and out in cold running water and pat dry. Season the chicken all around and inside the cavity with the salt, pepper, and 2 teaspoons of the seasoning mix. Dust the chicken all around with the flour.

3. Place the chicken in a large baking dish with a lid and add the cream of celery soup and water. Add the onion and celery to the liquid in the pan along with the remaining 1 teaspoon seasoning mix and the butter. Cover and bake for 30 minutes, then add the washed rice, mix well, cover, and bake for 20 minutes more.

4. Check the rice. It should be cooked through but with plenty of liquid remaining, thick and soupy, not clumped and sticky. Remove the lid and continue to bake until the chicken skin is browned, about 15 minutes more.

5. Remove from the oven and allow the chicken to rest for 10 minutes, then remove the chicken from the dish and carve it. Place the carved chicken on top of the rice in the baking dish and serve hot from the dish.

miss robbie says . . . put it on rewind If you want to make this dish healthier, you can use ¼ cup extra virgin olive oil instead of butter. For the best-tasting dish, make sure to use the best quality olive oil you can get.

CHICKEN AND DUMPLINGS

Our chicken and dumplings is a recipe that my mom brought with her to St. Louis from her home in Mississippi. It's the kind of meal that takes some time to prepare, and is well worth the effort.

The chicken is typically cooked in plain water or, maybe, chicken broth. I like to add a small bit of my cream of celery soup for more flavor, and I use a whole chicken so the bones can further boost the flavor. To lighten the dish up you can substitute 3 pounds of skinless chicken breasts. If only using breasts, reduce the amount of water in the recipe by 1 quart. My dumplings are a bit like broad egg noodles in shape. I call for adding a little butter or oil to the pot before dropping the dumplings one at a time into the boiling liquid; this keeps them from clumping together.

SERVES 6

CHICKEN

1 (3-pound) chicken

1 small onion, chopped

1 stalk celery, minced

1 teaspoon salt

1 teaspoon ground black
  pepper

¼ cup Cream of Celery Soup
  (page 5)

2 tablespoons unsalted butter

DUMPLINGS

1½ cups all-purpose flour,
  plus more as needed

½ teaspoon baking powder

1 teaspoon salt

½ teaspoon ground black
  pepper

½ teaspoon No-Salt
  Seasoning Mix (page 182)

2 large egg yolks

1. In a stockpot, combine the chicken, onion, celery, salt, and pepper. Add 4 quarts of water and place over high heat until it comes to a boil. Stir in the cream of celery soup, then reduce the heat and simmer, uncovered, until the chicken is tender enough to pull easily from the bone and the liquid is reduced by half, 1 to 1 ½ hours.

2. Remove the chicken from the pot, cool slightly, and pull the meat from the bones. Discard the bones and skin, then return the chicken to the pot. Strain 1 cup of the chicken stock from the pot and set aside to cool for making the dumplings.

3. Make the dumplings: In a large bowl, whisk together the flour, baking powder, salt, pepper, and seasoning mix. Make a well in the center, add the egg yolks to the well, and beat them with a fork until they are frothy. Add the cooled reserved chicken broth to the egg yolks and beat together well.

4. Gradually pull the flour in from the sides of the well into the center and beat until the flour is completely mixed with the egg yolks and broth.

5. Turn the dough out onto a well-floured work surface and knead in more flour until the dough is stretchy and firm, about 4 to 5 minutes. Roll out the dough into a very thin square that measures about 13 x 13 inches. Cut the dough square in 6 equal

pieces so you have long rectangles, then cut each rectangle into 4 or 5 squares. Set them aside on the floured work surface.

6. Bring the chicken mixture back up to a boil and add the butter. Stir until the butter is melted, then add the dumplings one at a time and boil until the dumplings rise to the top of the pan, about 1 to 2 minutes.

7. Spoon the chicken and dumplings into large bowls and serve.

FRIED CHICKEN

This is my mama's fried chicken recipe. Her secret to tender chicken was to marinate it in seasoned buttermilk. We had fried chicken about once a week, and now that I think back on it, it's amazing that one chicken fed all nine of us. Everyone had to pick a different piece each week to be fair. Some weeks I got a wing, which wasn't much meat, but if I was lucky it was my turn to get a leg or, better yet, a breast. The breast was my favorite because it has the most meat, and I'm greedy. My mom served her fried chicken with creamed sweet peas and mashed potatoes. Serve as part of the Fried Chicken Dinner Menu (page 193).

SERVES 4 TO 6

1 (3-pound) chicken, cut into 8 pieces

1 tablespoon plus 2 teaspoons salt

2 teaspoons garlic powder

1 teaspoon ground black pepper

¼ teaspoon cayenne pepper

2 cups buttermilk

2½ cups all-purpose flour

½ teaspoon paprika

2 cups vegetable oil

1. Wash the chicken by putting it in a large bowl and rubbing 1 tablespoon of the salt all over it. Rinse under cold water, then transfer the chicken to another large bowl.

2. Season the chicken with 1 teaspoon of the remaining salt, 1 teaspoon of the garlic powder, ½ teaspoon of the black pepper, and the cayenne pepper.

3. Add the buttermilk to the chicken and turn each piece so it is well coated. Cover the bowl with plastic wrap and refrigerate for at least 4 hours or, better yet, overnight.

4. In a large bowl, whisk together the flour, the remaining 1 teaspoon garlic powder, the remaining ½ teaspoon black pepper, the remaining 1 teaspoon salt, and the paprika.

5. Take the chicken out of the refrigerator. One piece at a time, shake off excess buttermilk, dredge the chicken pieces in the flour mixture, and place on a plate. For a crispier coating, you can dip each piece in the buttermilk and flour again.

6. Once all the chicken is floured up, put the plate back in the refrigerator for about 30 minutes.

7. Heat the oil in a large deep skillet, preferably cast-iron, over medium heat. Drop a little flour in the skillet; if the flour bubbles hard, then the oil is ready.

8. Gently lay each piece of chicken in the skillet, leaving about ½ inch around each piece—don't crowd them. You may need

to fry the chicken in two batches. Cover the pan and fry the chicken, lifting the cover and turning once, until both sides are golden brown, about 15 minutes per side. If you like your chicken a lighter brown, fry it for 8 to 10 minutes per side, then put the pieces on a baking sheet and finish it off in a preheated 350°F oven for 20 minutes.

miss robbie says . . . put it on rewind   If you want to lighten up your fried chicken, bake it instead of frying it. Spray a cookie sheet and the top of the chicken lightly with cooking spray. Arrange the chicken pieces on the sheet so they aren't overlapping or touching. Bake in a preheated 400°F oven for 30 minutes, or until the pieces are nicely browned.

miss robbie says . . . do a punch-in   If you have leftover fried chicken pieces, a great way to use them up is to smother them; check out my smothered chicken recipe on page 60.

ROAST TURKEY WITH GRAVY

Thanksgiving is my holiday, and I do most of the cooking—from the turkey to the fixings, and that includes cornbread dressing, chitterlings, greens, macaroni and cheese, candied yams, spaghetti, coleslaw, chess pie, sweet potato pie, caramel cake, and several other kinds of cake (have a look at the full menu on page 194). Linda makes the potato salad and Jan brings the baked beans.

Thanksgiving is dear to my heart because for too many years, it was a catch as catch can holiday. When I was on the road with the Ikettes and after, we'd have Thanksgiving in a restaurant. If we were lucky enough to be on break in Los Angeles we'd put together a home-cooked meal, but it wasn't anything like being home with family.

Nowadays at Sweetie Pie's we go crazy sharing the holiday with everyone. The restaurant is closed that day, so we can get together with our best customers and the staff around five or so—after everyone has had a chance to see their families. We set up the meal buffet-style, and we make so much food that we never run out.

After everyone has fixed a plate, we play music and dance, and we have a lot of fun telling jokes. Every year I'm amazed by how many people come, and every year I feel more blessed than the last.

When you make turkey for your own celebration, it is most important to keep it from becoming dry. The way to do it is to rub the turkey with butter and cook it in a roasting bag with some extra liquid, preferably my Onion Soup (page 3). I don't stuff my bird before roasting, which allows it to cook evenly and shortens the cooking time. I serve my turkey with Cornbread Dressing (page 118).

SERVES 6 TO 8

1 (12- to 14-pound) turkey, giblets reserved

1 teaspoon salt

2 teaspoons ground black pepper

3 tablespoons No-Salt Seasoning Mix (page 182)

½ cup (1 stick) unsalted butter, softened

2 medium onions, roughly chopped

4 stalks celery, trimmed and roughly chopped

1 quart chicken stock

2 cups onion soup (page 3)

Turkey Gravy (recipe follows)

1. Preheat the oven to 325°F.

2. Wash the turkey inside and out under cold running water and pat dry. Season the turkey evenly outside and in the cavity with the salt, pepper, and seasoning mix.

3. Using your fingers or a small paring knife, gently pull the skin away from the breast and rub half the butter under the skin, then rub the remaining butter all over the rest of the bird.

4. Put the onions and celery in the cavity along with the giblets. Place the bird in an oven-roasting bag for turkey and place the bagged bird in a roasting pan large enough to hold it.

5. Gently pour the chicken stock and onion soup into the bag and tie it up.

6. Put the turkey in the middle of the oven and roast for 3 to 3½ hours, depending on the size of your bird. The rule is generally 15 minutes per pound unstuffed.

7. When the bird registers 165°F on a meat thermometer pushed into the thickest part of the thigh, cut open the bag and take it out—be careful not to get a steam burn. Let the turkey rest for about 15 minutes before carving. You can use the liquid in the bag for gravy.

TURKEY GRAVY

Since I cook my turkey in a roasting bag with extra liquid, there are always plenty of good drippings. I use at least a cup of the drippings to make my Cornbread Dressing (page 118) and the rest to make savory gravy. You'll want to strain the liquid from the roasting pan into another pan so that it's smooth and clear.

Liquid from roasting 1 turkey
  (page 37), strained
¼ cup cornstarch
¼ cup water
Salt and pepper

1. Pour the strained roasting liquid into a medium saucepan and place over medium heat.

2. In a small bowl, whisk the cornstarch into water until the cornstarch is dissolved and the mixture looks like heavy cream.

3. When the roasting liquid comes to a simmer, add the cornstarch mixture and whisk it well. Raise the heat to high, bring to a boil, then quickly lower the heat. Keep on whisking until the gravy is thick enough to coat the back of a spoon.

4. Taste for seasoning and adjust it if it's not to your liking. Serve with your roasted turkey.

TURKEY AND NOODLES

Turkey wings are more available in the grocery store than ever before—without buying the whole turkey. While this recipe starts with raw wings, turkey and noodles is also great dish to make with leftover Thanksgiving turkey, and it's quick to put together. When the turkey is already cooked, you can reduce the baking time to 15 minutes at the most before adding the noodles. Turkey wings are pretty big, so figure on just one for each person.

SERVES 6

6 turkey wings with drumettes

1 teaspoon salt

1 teaspoon ground black pepper

3 teaspoons No-Salt Seasoning Mix (page 182)

1 tablespoon all-purpose flour

4 cups Cream of Celery Soup (page 5)

2 cups water

1 medium onion, chopped

2 stalks celery, chopped

4 tablespoons (½ stick) unsalted butter, cut in half

1 bag egg noodles

1. Preheat the oven to 375°F.

2. If using raw turkey wings, wash them under cold running water and pat dry. Season the turkey wings with the salt, pepper, and 2 teaspoons of the seasoning mix. Dust the wings with the flour. If you are using precooked turkey wings go on to Step 3.

3. Place the chicken in a large baking dish with a lid and add the cream of celery soup and water. Add the onion and celery to the liquid in the baking dish along with the remaining 1 teaspoon seasoning mix and the butter.

4. Bake, covered, for 30 minutes, then add the egg noodles and bake for 10 to 15 minutes more, until the noodles are cooked through but there is still plenty of liquid remaining. Remove the cover and bake for another 15 minutes, or until the turkey wings begin to brown. Remove from the oven and serve immediately.

MR. JOHN'S QUARTERED DUCK ON FRIED RICE

I used to order Mr. John's Quartered Duck from a restaurant in St. Louis. The guy who ran the place was called Mr. John, and the dish had a sort of a Chinese flair to it. The rice was fried and the duck was roasted and seasoned with soy sauce. For years I kept trying to figure out Mr. John's recipe, and finally I came up with this version. To really make it work, the rice should be cooked and refrigerated, which makes this dish a great way to use up day-old rice. Duck can be greasy, so I always cook my duck on a rack over a baking pan to reduce the fat.

SERVES 4

1 (3-pound) duck

1 teaspoon salt

1 teaspoon ground black pepper

1 teaspoon No-Salt Seasoning Mix (page 182)

2 cups chicken stock

1 tablespoon canola oil

1 small onion, minced

1 medium green bell pepper, cored, seeded, and minced

2 cups cooked white rice

3 tablespoons soy sauce

1 large egg, beaten

1. Preheat the oven to 425°F. Wash the duck well under cold running water both inside the cavity and out. Pat dry.

2. Put the duck on a wire rack set over a deep broiler pan or baking dish and use a sharp paring knife to make crisscross cuts in the skin. Season the duck with the salt, pepper, and no-salt seasoning mix and bake uncovered for 2 hours, or until a meat thermometer inserted into the deepest part of the thigh comes up at 165°F. You might have to ladle out some of the duck fat from the pan now and then while it's cooking so the fat doesn't overflow.

3. Remove the duck from the oven and let it rest for 15 to 20 minutes, until it's cool enough to handle. Then cut the duck into quarters, two pieces containing a breast and wing and two with a leg and thigh.

4. Combine the chicken stock and 2 tablespoons of soy sauce in a large saucepan and add the duck quarters. Place over medium-high heat, bring to a simmer, then reduce the heat and simmer until almost all the liquid is gone, 15 to 20 minutes.

5. Meanwhile, heat the oil in a large skillet over medium heat. Add the onion and bell pepper and cook until softened, about 5 minutes, then add the rice and mix it in well. Stir in the remaining soy sauce.

6. Add the beaten egg and allow to sit for a minute or so, until it firms up, then mix well. Put the fried rice on a platter and arrange the duck quarters on top of it.

BAKED HAM

Honey ham is easy to fix, especially if you start with a precooked ham. We serve ham on Easter and on Mother's Day, with Candied Carrot Soufflé (page 99), Potato Salad (page 14), and Mixed Greens (page 87) or Roasted Brussels Sprouts with Garlic and Bacon (page 116) alongside. A cold ham sandwich is a favorite of mine, and it's excellent on Roberta's Grandmother's Yeast Rolls (page 128) with mayonnaise.

SERVES 10 TO 12

1 bone-in cooked ham (on
  average 12 pounds)
10 to 20 whole cloves
1 (8-ounce) can pineapple
  slices
1 (4-ounce) bottle maraschino
  cherries
½ cup honey

1. Preheat the oven to 350°F.

2. Place the ham in a deep baking dish or roasting pan and use a sharp knife to make crisscross marks all around the surface. Press the cloves, pointed side down, into the cross marks all around the ham. Cover the pan with foil, put it in the oven, and bake for 15 to 20 minutes, until it's heated through.

3. While the ham is heating, pour the juice off the pineapple slices into a medium bowl; reserve the pineapple slices. Pour the juice off the maraschino cherries into the bowl and reserve the cherries. Add the honey and whisk to dissolve the honey.

4. Remove the ham from the oven and arrange the pineapple slices around the ham. Using a toothpick, spear a maraschino cherry and place it in the center of one of the pineapple slices, pushing it down to secure it into the ham. Repeat until all the pineapple slices are filled with cherries.

5. Drizzle the dressed ham with one third of the pineapple-honey mixture, cover it again, and put it back in the oven for another 20 minutes, drizzling it with the honey mixture 2 or 3 more times.

6. Remove the foil from the ham and bake until the pineapple slices to start to brown, about 10 minutes. Remove from the oven and allow to rest for 10 minutes, then pull the toothpicks out of the cherries. Slice and serve with your choice of sides.

PORK ROAST

Pork roast is another one of those meals my mom would fix on a Sunday. Her pork roast recipe isn't that different from the way she fixed roast beef, so really, it's all about whether you like the flavor of pork or beef more. Apples go really well with pork, so you can slice up a few peeled Granny Smith apples and toss them in with the vegetables, if you like.

SERVES 6 TO 8

1 (3-pound) pork roast

Salt and pepper

1 teaspoon all-purpose flour

2 tablespoons unsalted butter or margarine, softened

4 cups Onion Soup (page 3)

2 pounds baby red bliss potatoes

1 medium onion, thinly sliced

2 stalks celery, chopped

3 carrots, chopped

2 Granny Smith apples, peeled, cored, and cut into 6 wedges

2 tablespoons cornstarch

2 tablespoons water

1. Preheat the oven to 325°F.

2. Wash the roast under cold running water and pat it dry. Season it real well with salt and pepper.

3. Dust a large roasting bag with the flour. Place the roast in an oven-safe roasting bag, smear the softened butter all over the top of the roast, then pour in the onion soup.

4. Seal up the bag loosely and roast for 1 to 1¼ hours, then carefully open the bag (so you don't get a steam burn) and add the potatoes, onion, celery, carrots, and apples and roast for another 30 minutes, or until a meat thermometer comes up at 145°F for medium-rare.

5. Remove the roast and place it on a platter to rest. Use a slotted spoon to remove the vegetables and arrange them around the roast.

6. Pour the cooking liquid through a fine-mesh strainer into a saucepan and bring it to a boil. In a small bowl, whisk the cornstarch into the water until the cornstarch is dissolved and the mixture resembles heavy cream. Add the cornstarch slurry to the liquid in the pan and whisk until the gravy thickens. Serve the roast with the gravy on the side, along with a green vegetable.

onion soup in a hurry Some of the recipes in this book—like this pork roast, Sunday Fresh Fried Corn (page 101), and Sunday Roast Beef (page 74)—call for liquid onion soup. If you don't have it on hand, you can use my Over-the-Top Homemade Onion Soup Mix: stir 1 tablespoon of the mix into each cup of water and simmer over medium heat. When the mix is dissolved, you've got onion soup to use how you like—or just to sip straight!

STUFFED PORK CHOPS

Stuffed pork chops are real comfort food, especially if you stuff them with cornbread or another bread dressing. Rice makes another great option for stuffing your chops. The key is to use a thick-cut pork shop—at least 3 inches thick—and one chop will make a good meal for a person with an average appetite. I like to serve my stuffed pork chops with Mashed Potatoes (page 112) and Lima Beans (page 81) alongside.

SERVES 4

4 (8-ounce) center-cut, bone-in pork chops
1½ cups Cornbread Dressing (page 118)
Salt and pepper
No-Salt Seasoning Mix (page 182)
½ cup regular or low-sodium chicken stock
1 tablespoon unsalted butter

1. Preheat the oven to 325°F.

2. Use a paring knife to make a slit about 2 inches wide and 2 inches deep in the side of each pork chop. This is where you'll put the stuffing.

3. Divide the stuffing into 4 equal portions, then stuff each portion into the cuts you've made in the chops.

4. Season the pork chops with salt, pepper, and no-salt seasoning mix very well on all sides. Be careful to keep the stuffing from falling out.

5. Lay the pork chops in an oven-safe dish with a lid. They can fit closely, but they shouldn't be snug or crowded. Add the chicken stock and butter.

6. Cover the dish and bake for 30 to 40 minutes, until the pork chops are firm and register 160°F when tested with a meat thermometer, removing the cover for the last 5 minutes of cooking to brown them up a little.

SWEETIE PIE'S TENDER OVEN-BAKED ST. LOUIS-STYLE BBQ RIBS

Folks in St. Louis pride themselves on their ribs. You could say it's the city's signature dish. Growing up in the projects like we did, we didn't have a barbecue pit or a smoker, so when we wanted ribs, my mom came up with this way of doing them in the oven. Another way she'd make her ribs was to cut the rack into small slabs of two or three ribs, marinate and season them, and then fry them up—just like you'd do a pork chop. Serve with Potato Salad (page 14) or Mac and Cheese (page 109).

SERVES 4 TO 6

2 to 4 pounds boneless pork ribs (you could also use beef)

1 cup pineapple juice, unsweetened

2 teaspoons salt

1 teaspoon ground black pepper

2 teaspoons sugar

1 teaspoon paprika

About 1½ cups water

1 cup Barbecue Sauce (page 184)

1. Preheat the oven to 250°F.

2. Wash the ribs under cold running water and pat them dry.

3. Put the ribs in a large deep dish and pour the pineapple juice over it. Cover and marinate in the refrigerator for at least 4 hours, preferably overnight.

4. Whisk together the salt, pepper, sugar, and paprika in a large baking dish. Roll the ribs in the mixture, then arrange them in the baking dish. Add enough water to come halfway up the sides of the baking pan.

5. Bake the ribs for about 1 hour or until they are no longer pink when the meat is sliced away from the bone, then remove them from the oven and drain. Add the barbecue sauce and toss the ribs evenly to coat.

6. Increase the oven temperature to 400°F and return the baking dish to the oven. Bake for 20 to 30 minutes. Remove from the heat and serve.

NECK BONES THREE WAYS

Pork neck bones are very common in a black household—right along with chitterlings. These types of foods are based on what I call "rootie to tootie" eating—meaning that you eat the whole part of the animal from its nose to its tail and everything in between.

Nowadays a lot of famous chefs are pushing exactly this type of cuisine, but in the historical black experience, there wasn't really much choice but to eat in this way. What started out as "slave food," in other words, those foods that weren't considered good enough for the slave owners, became part of a traditional way of cooking.

I make neck bones three ways: boiled, baked, and barbecued. While the methods differ, the recipes for each are quite similar, with the barbecue sauce adding a different kind of flavoring.

The easiest way to clean neck bones is to soak them in very cold water. Make sure to take the time to remove the membranes from the bones because they can become tough and rubbery when cooked.

There's not a lot of meat on neck bones, and they have to be cooked a fairly long time for the meat to become tender. The best way to eat neck bones is the old-school way: pick them up with your fingers and suck on the bone.

BOILED NECK BONES

SERVES 4 TO 6

4 pounds pork neck bones,
    membrane and marrow
    removed
2 teaspoons salt
1 teaspoon ground black pepper
½ cup onion soup mix,
    homemade (page 183) or store-
    bought
3 stalks celery, chopped
1 large onion, chopped
4 white potatoes, peeled and
    diced

1. Place the cleaned neck bones in a large deep pot and fill the pot halfway with water. Place over high heat and bring to a boil, skimming off any foam that rises to the top. Keep skimming until there's no more foam, then reduce the heat to medium-low.

2. Add the salt, pepper, onion soup mix, celery, and onion, cover, and simmer until the liquid is reduced by three-quarters, 1½ to 2 hours, adding the potatoes during the last 30 minutes of cooking.

3. Remove from the heat and serve immediately with a little of the broth, perhaps with Smothered Cabbage (page 90) alongside.

BAKED NECK BONES

SERVES 4 TO 6

4 pounds pork neck bones,
  membrane and marrow
  removed
2 teaspoons salt
1 teaspoon ground black pepper
½ cup onion soup mix,
  homemade (page 183) or store-
  bought
3 stalks celery, chopped
1 large onion, chopped
4 white potatoes, peeled and
  diced
2 teaspoons No-Salt Seasoning
  Mix (page 182)

1. Preheat the oven to 275°F.

2. Place the cleaned neck bones in a large deep baking dish with a cover. Add the salt, pepper, onion soup mix, celery, and onion and cover the dish. Bake for 1½ to 2 hours, then add the potatoes and seasoning mix.

3. Cover and bake for an additional 30 minutes, or until the potatoes are tender, then, remove the cover and bake until the neck bones and potatoes start to brown, about 20 more minutes, and the meat can easily pull away from the bone using a fork. Remove from the oven and serve immediately.

BARBECUED NECK BONES

SERVES 4 TO 6

4 pounds pork neck bones,
  membrane and marrow
  removed
2 teaspoons salt
1 teaspoon ground black pepper
½ cup onion soup mix,
  homemade (page 183) or store-
  bought
3 stalks celery, chopped
1 large onion, chopped
4 white potatoes, peeled and
  diced
2 teaspoons No-Salt Seasoning
  Mix (page 182)
¾ cup Barbecue Sauce
  (page 184)
2 teaspoons sugar

1. Preheat the oven to 275°F.

2. Place the cleaned neck bones in a large deep baking dish with a cover. Add the salt, pepper, onion soup mix, celery, and onion and cover the dish. Bake for 1½ to 2 hours, then add the potatoes and seasoning mix.

3. Cover and bake for an additional 30 minutes, or until the potatoes are tender, then remove the cover, brush the neck bones with the barbecue sauce, and sprinkle them evenly with the sugar.

4. Keep the cover off and bake until the neck bones and potatoes start to brown, about 20 minutes, and the meat can easily pull away from the bone using a fork. Remove from the oven and serve immediately.

CHITTERLINGS (AKA CHITLINS)

You might be wondering why I include chitlins in this book. There's probably no other soul food that has been talked about and talked over and argued about than chitlins.

For those of you who don't know, chitlins (or, actually, chitterlings) are pig intestines, and back in the day they were one of those throwaway parts of the animals that were thought to be only good enough for slaves and, later, for poor black folk. Maybe it's that fact that makes some people shy away from chitlins, but the truth is they are a solid part of our food history and we shouldn't forget them—even if we do only eat them once in a while.

Nowadays, folks who call themselves "gourmet" say it's right to eat every part of the animal. Well, that's nothing new to soul-food cooking—you cooked what you got and made the best of it—from rootie to tootie, as I always say.

Having said all of that, I'll also say that not many cooks today can turn out a good pot of chitlins and it's a dish I won't eat just anywhere. It's true that they can surely smell when you're cooking them—that's why you have to clean them well. And they need to cook for a long time over low heat—at least three or four hours. As with a lot of things, I use my onion soup mix, red pepper flakes, and hot sauce to add flavor and give my special kind of soul to the recipe.

I'll tell you one thing: If you learn how to make a good pot of chitlins then, just like my own favorite song by Al Hibber says, "You'll Never Walk Alone."

MAKES 10 POUNDS

8 or 9 pounds of chitlins

About ⅓ cup coarse salt

3 tablespoons No-Salt Seasoning Mix (page 182)

½ teaspoon red pepper flakes

½ cup onion soup mix, homemade (page 183) or store-bought

1 small onion, chopped

1 small potato, peeled and cut in half (optional)

1 teaspoon hot sauce, or more to taste

1. Put the chitterlings in a large bowl and add cold water to cover. Take each chitterling out and pull the membrane away from the inside; you may have to put a cut in the membrane in order to pull it off. Discard the membranes.

2. Rinse the cleaned chitterlings well in the bowl of cold water, then drain them.

3. Sprinkle the chitterlings with the coarse salt and rub it in well. Add enough cold water to cover and swirl it around. Pour off the water and rinse the chitterlings one more time in cold water. Drain well. If you see any scum or grit coming off the chitterlings, then keep on washing them until the water runs clear—this is important. There will be water residue in the bowl; this is fine. Don't dump it out.

4. Place the chitterlings in a stockpot along with any remain-

ing water left in the bowl. Add the salt, seasoning mix, pepper flakes, onion soup mix, onion, and potato, if using. Some folks believe adding the potato helps with the smell, but if you clean the chitterlings membrane as I do, the smell won't be an issue.

5. Place over high heat, bring to a simmer, then reduce the heat to low and simmer for 3 to 4 hours. The chitterlings will release their own liquid to cook in, so don't add more. They're done when you can use a fork to break them up; you want to break them up into ½-inch pieces. Stir in the hot sauce right before serving.

LIVER AND ONIONS

My dad loved to fix liver and onions and kidneys and rice. He also liked mountain oysters—which are actually sheep testicles.

The way we do liver and onions is to smother it. If you don't care for thick gravy, you could fry up your liver, then fry the onions in the leftover grease and spread them on top. The key is to start with a hot oiled skillet, sear off that liver quickly, then take it out of the pan, as this is a cut of meat that cooks up pretty quickly.

I serve my liver and onions with rice, Smothered Potatoes (page 111), or Mashed Potatoes (page 112).

SERVES 4

1 calf or beef liver

Salt and pepper

¼ cup plus 2 tablespoons
   all-purpose flour

5 tablespoons vegetable oil

3 medium onions, sliced into
   thin rings

4 tablespoons onion soup
   mix, homemade (page 183)
   or store-bought

2 cups hot water

1. Lay the liver on a cutting board and spread it out flat. Season both sides very well with salt and pepper.

2. Spread ¼ cup of the flour out on a wide plate or platter and lightly dredge the liver in it. Shake off any excess.

3. Heat 3 tablespoons of the oil in a large skillet over high heat until the oil is hot but not smoking. Add the liver and sear it on one side until it's lightly browned, 1 to 2 minutes, then gently turn it over and sear for another 1 to 2 minutes. Take the liver out of the pan and set it on a large plate.

4. Lower the heat to medium and add the remaining 2 tablespoons vegetable oil, then add the remaining 2 tablespoons flour. Cook, stirring constantly, until the flour colors to a medium-dark brown, about 2 minutes. Add the onions and cook, stirring constantly, until they begin to soften, 2 to 3 minutes, then stir in the onion soup mix.

5. Add the hot water and stir or whisk it in well, bring to a simmer, and simmer until the mixture gets good and thick like gravy, then add back the liver and simmer for 6 to 7 minutes or until the liver is very firm. Cover and let it sit for a minute more; don't leave it too long or it will become tough. Serve the liver and onions over rice, smothered potatoes, or mashed potatoes.

get smothered

Smothering meat in lots of onions and gravy adds rich flavor. When we were growing up it was seen as making something out of nothing. For my mom, it was an economical way to feed our big family—anything smothered filled you up and made you think you had more meat. You can smother just about any kind or cut of meat—the technique is always the same—only the cooking time will change based on the kind of meat you're cooking. There is one rule of thumb when it comes to smothering—the more onions the better!

SMOTHERED PORK CHOPS

SERVES 4

4 center-cut, bone-in pork
chops
Salt and pepper
1 cup vegetable oil
1 medium onion, thinly
sliced
¼ cup all-purpose flour
1½ cups water

1. Season the pork chops well with salt and pepper—don't be stingy.

2. Heat the oil in a large, deep skillet over medium heat. Lay the pork chops in the pan, but take care not to crowd them (cook them up in two batches if necessary). Fry the pork chops for 8 to 10 minutes, until golden brown, then turn over and brown on the other side, another 8 to 10 minutes.

3. Remove the pork chops and set them aside on a plate. Use a spoon to remove all but 1 tablespoon of grease from the skillet. Add the onions and cook until they are softened and golden, about 5 minutes.

4. Add the flour and cook, stirring, for 1 to 2 minutes, until the flour becomes golden brown. Add the water and mix well so you can scrape up the browned bits at the bottom of the pan.

5. Return the pork chops to the pan and reduce the heat to medium-low. Cover and simmer for 10 minutes more, or until the chops are cooked through and the sauce is nice and thick. Taste the gravy and season it again if needed. If necessary, you can use two skillets, dividing the gravy and onions between them before adding back the pork chops. Serve with Mashed Potatoes (page 112).

SMOTHERED CUBE STEAK

2 pounds cube steak

Salt and pepper

1 tablespoon vegetable oil

1 medium onion, thinly sliced

¼ cup all-purpose flour

1½ cups water

1. Season the steak well with salt and pepper.

2. Heat a large, deep skillet over medium and add the oil. Lay the steak in the pan and cook for 12 to 14 minutes, until browned, then turn it over and brown the other side, another 12 to 14 minutes.

3. Remove the steak from the skillet and set it aside on a plate. Use a spoon to remove all but 1 tablespoon of the grease from the skillet. Add the onion and cook until softened and golden, about 5 minutes.

4. Add the flour and cook, stirring, for 1 to 2 minutes, until the flour becomes golden brown. Add the water and mix well so you can scrape up the browned bits at the bottom of the pan.

5. Return the steak to the pan and reduce heat to medium-low. Cover and simmer for 10 minutes more, or until sauce is nice and thick. Serve with Mashed Potatoes (page 112).

SMOTHERED SALISBURY STEAKS

1½ pounds lean ground
  beef
1 tablespoon vegetable oil
1 medium onion, thinly
  sliced
1 large green bell pepper,
  cored, seeded, and thinly
  sliced
½ cup all-purpose flour
1½ cups water

1. Form the meat into 4 oval patties about 5 inches long and 4 inches across.

2. Heat the oil in a large, deep skillet over medium heat. Lay the patties in the pan, taking care not to crowd them (cook them in batches if needed). Fry the patties for 6 to 8 minutes on each side, until they are firm and hold their shape.

3. Remove the patties from the skillet and set them on a plate. Use a spoon to remove all but 1 tablespoon of grease from the skillet. Add the onion and bell pepper and sauté until they are soft and colored, about 5 minutes.

4. Add the flour and cook, stirring, for 1 to 2 minutes, until the flour becomes golden brown. Add the water and mix well so you can scrape up the browned bits at the bottom of the pan.

5. Return the Salisbury steaks back to the pan and reduce the heat to medium-low. Cover and simmer for 10 minutes, or until the steaks are cooked through and the gravy is nice and thick. If necessary, you can use two pans, dividing the gravy between them before adding back the steaks. Serve with Mashed Potatoes (page 112) or Roasted Brussels Sprouts with Garlic and Bacon (page 106).

SMOTHERED CHICKEN

I make my smothered chicken with a sauce that's a little different from the typical brown sauce that goes with red meat. I use cream of celery soup, which is lighter and goes nicely with chicken. You may want to fry the chicken without breading it, or you can prepare it like you would my Fried Chicken (page 35), and then follow the directions for smothering it. In fact, leftover fried chicken works really well in this recipe.

SERVES 4

2 pounds skinless bone-
  in chicken thighs, or
  2 pounds leftover fried or
  roasted chicken
Salt and pepper
2 tablespoons vegetable oil
1 tablespoon all-purpose
  flour
1 medium onion, thinly
  sliced
1½ cups cream of celery
  soup
½ cup hot water
1 cup parboiled rice
1 tablespoon unsalted
  butter

1. Preheat the oven to 350°F.

2. Wash the chicken under cold running water and pat it dry. Season the pieces well with salt and pepper.

3. Heat 1 tablespoon of the oil in a large, deep ovenproof pot, preferably cast-iron. Lay the chicken thighs in the pan, taking care not to crowd them, and cook for 6 to 8 minutes per side, until they are nicely browned. Remove the chicken thighs from the pot and set them on a plate.

4. Add the flour and cook, stirring, until it's golden brown, 1 to 2 minutes. Add the onion and cook until softened, about 3 minutes.

5. Stir in the cream of celery soup and hot water. Cook, stirring, for 1 to 2 minutes, scraping up any browned bits at the bottom of the pan. Season the gravy with salt and pepper.

6. Return the chicken thighs to the pan along with the rice and butter.

7. Cover the pan, place it in the oven, and bake for 15 to 20 minutes, until the chicken is cooked through and the rice absorbs most of the liquid.

BEEF CHILI

Chili is a dish that tastes better the next day. I like to make a big pot so the first day I can have it with crackers or a piece of Hot Water Cornbread (page 121) and the next day I can serve it over spaghetti or rice. You'll see that I put a little sugar in my chili, but if you are watching your sugar or don't care for that touch of sweetness, you can certainly leave it out. Substitute turkey for the beef for a lower-fat alternative.

SERVES 6 TO 8

2 teaspoons vegetable oil

1 medium onion, minced

1 large green bell pepper, cored, seeded, and chopped

1 (6-ounce) can tomato paste

2 pounds 80% lean ground beef or ground turkey

4 cups canned chili beans

4 cups canned diced tomatoes

1 teaspoon ground cumin

1 teaspoon chili powder

1 teaspoon salt

1 tablespoon sugar

2 tablespoons hot sauce of your choice, or more to taste

1. Heat the oil in a large cast-iron pot or Dutch oven over medium heat. Add the onion and bell pepper and cook, stirring, until they start to soften, about 2 minutes, then stir in half of the tomato paste and cook, stirring, for 1 minute.

2. Add the ground beef and stir to coat it in the tomato paste mixture, then add the beans.

3. Add the diced tomatoes with their liquid, the cumin, chili powder, salt, and sugar and bring to a simmer. Cover the pot, reduce the heat to low, and simmer for 1 hour, stirring occasionally.

4. Remove the cover, stir in the hot sauce, and cook uncovered for 10 minutes more. Serve with crackers, plain spaghetti, or cornbread, or try serving it over tamales.

BEEF ENCHILADAS

My beef enchiladas and other Mexican-inspired recipes are influenced by my time in Los Angeles. You'll see a few Mexican-style recipes in this book like my Soulful Taco (page 19), Tamale Pie (page 73), and this enchilada and enchilada sauce. That's because I lived in Los Angeles for nearly twenty years and there is a strong Mexican food influence there. If you like hot sauce, as I do, you can add it to the stuffed enchiladas before you roll them up.

SERVES 6

1 pound 80% lean ground beef or ground turkey

2 medium onions, minced

1 medium green bell pepper, cored, seeded, and finely chopped

Salt and pepper

6 large flour tortillas

2 cups shredded Colby cheese

2 cups shredded Monterey Jack cheese

2 cups Enchilada Sauce (page 185)

Hot sauce for serving (optional)

Raw minced onion for garnish (optional)

1. Preheat the oven to 350°F.

2. Heat a large skillet over medium heat and add the ground beef. Cook, stirring to break up the pieces, until the beef is browned, about 15 minutes. Add half of the onions and the bell pepper and cook, stirring, for 5 minutes, until the onions and pepper soften. Season well with salt and pepper.

3. Using a slotted spoon, remove the ground meat mixture from the pan and put it in a bowl. In a separate bowl, combine the two cheeses.

4. Lay a large tortilla on a clean, flat surface and spoon about 3 tablespoons of the cheese mixture on one side of it. Next, add one sixth of the meat mixture on one side of the tortilla. Then add another 3 tablespoons of cheese on top of the meat.

5. Roll the tortilla away from you like a big cigar and put it in a baking dish, seam side down. Repeat until all the tortillas are filled and are arranged comfortably in the baking dish.

6. Sprinkle the enchiladas with half of the remaining cheese, then spread half of the enchilada sauce on top. Sprinkle the sauce with the remaining raw pepper and then the remaining sauce. Finish it off with the rest of the cheese.

7. Place in the oven and bake until the cheese is melted, bubbly, and beginning to brown. Serve immediately, with hot sauce and a garnish of raw onion, if you like.

MEATLOAF

Meatloaf goes with nearly everything—mashed potatoes, creamed peas, salad, greens, fried corn, rice, Brussels sprouts . . . the list goes on. Because I like to use the drippings from my meatloaf in the tomato sauce that I spread on top of it, I cook it as a freeform loaf rather than in a loaf pan, which makes the topping shiny and smooth.

Serve with Mashed Potatoes (page 112) or Mashed Rutabaga or Turnips (page 116).

SERVES 4

2 pounds 80% lean ground beef

6 tablespoons onion soup mix, homemade (page 183) or store-bought

2 small onions, minced

2 small green bell peppers, cored, seeded, and minced

10 saltines, crushed

½ cup milk

2 large eggs

1 tablespoon all-purpose flour

1 teaspoon salt, plus more to taste

½ teaspoon ground black pepper, plus more to taste

4 cups tomato sauce

3 tablespoons sugar

1. Preheat the oven to 400°F.

2. In a large bowl, mix together the ground beef, onion soup mix, onions, and bell peppers. Soak the saltines in the milk until they become mushy, then add them to the beef mixture. Using your hands, mix everything together very well, then add the eggs, flour, salt, and pepper and knead the mixture with your hands.

3. In a small bowl, combine the tomato sauce and sugar and season with salt and pepper.

4. Lightly spray a large baking dish with cooking spray and form the meat mixture into a wide, even loaf.

5. Bake for 30 minutes, then remove 3 tablespoons of the drippings from the pan and add it to the tomato sauce mixture. Spread the tomato sauce mixture over the top and sides of the meatloaf and bake for another 15 minutes. Serve with mashed potatoes and creamed peas.

miss robbie says . . . do a punch-in! You can also use this recipe to make meatballs. Shape the meat mixture into balls about the size of a tangerine. Heat a large skillet with 3 tablespoons olive oil, add the meatballs, and brown them lightly on all sides. Heat up about 2 cups of tomato sauce, season with salt and pepper, then gently add the browned meatballs to the sauce to finish cooking for about 15 minutes or so. Serve over spaghetti.

THE BIG MO (HAMBURGER)

On Saturdays my mother would send me down to the grocer to buy ten pounds of hamburger meat on special and we'd make burgers. They could be as big as you wanted and you could put whatever you wanted on them. I always made mine with chopped green peppers and onions, and ate them between two slices of Texas Toast that was browned up in a buttered skillet. Then I'd slather the toast with plenty of mayonnaise and add some sliced tomatoes and lettuce. I called it the Big Mo, and it was my favorite food. When you make yours, cut the add-ins real small and cook it low and slow. I like to experiment with a mix of vegetables like zucchini, carrots, and even celery. You can also change up the flavor by using a mixture of pork and beef or lamb and beef. Put the Big Mo on a hot grill in the summer, and you've got pure mm-mm goodness!

SERVES 8

2 pounds lean ground beef

1 small onion, finely minced

1 small red or green bell pepper, cored, seeded, and finely minced

1 teaspoon salt

½ teaspoon ground black pepper

½ teaspoon vegetable oil

1. In a large bowl, mix together all the ingredients except the oil using your hands.

2. Form the dough into 8 equal-size balls and flatten them into patties.

3. Heat the oil in a large skillet over low heat. Gently lay the burgers down on the skillet, but don't crowd them in the pan (work in batches). Give each burger about a ½ inch of breathing room around it.

5. Cook the burgers low and slow until they start to firm up, about 10 minutes, and then flip them over and cook for 10 minutes more.

6. Serve hot on Texas Toast or hamburger rolls, with lettuce, tomato, mayonnaise, ketchup, or whatever you like.

miss robbie says . . . put it on rewind! Using ground turkey or chicken will lighten up this recipe. As they cook quicker than beef, soften your vegetable add-ins by cooking them down a bit in a skillet coated with cooking spray until just tender.

BEEF SHORT RIBS

It was rare that we got to eat short ribs growing up because they were—and still are—fairly expensive. I don't cook my short ribs to the point where the meat falls off the bone, but I do like to cook them long enough so that the tough membrane around the bone gets tender, which takes two to three hours. Short ribs make a pretty heavy meal, so I like to stick with a light side such as salad or some boiled carrots tossed in a little bit of melted butter and seasoned simply with salt and pepper.

SERVES 4

2 pounds beef short ribs

Salt and pepper

All-purpose flour for dredging

1 tablespoon vegetable oil

1 medium onion, finely chopped

2 stalks celery, finely chopped

1 medium green bell pepper, cored, seeded, and finely chopped

2 cups water

4 medium yellow potatoes, chopped

2 carrots, chopped

3 tablespoons onion soup mix, homemade (page 183) or store-bought

1. Preheat the oven to 350°F.

2. Wash the short ribs under cold running cold water and pat dry. Season the ribs well with salt and pepper, then dredge them lightly in flour, shaking off any excess.

3. Heat the oil in a large skillet over medium heat. Add the short ribs and brown them on all sides, about 2 minutes per side, then remove them from the skillet to a deep ovenproof baking dish.

4. Add the onion, celery, and bell pepper to the dish along with the water. Cover and bake for 2 hours.

5. Add the potatoes and carrots along with the onion soup mix. Cover the dish again and return to the oven for 45 minutes more. Remove the lid and let the vegetables brown for 15 minutes. Serve immediately.

STUFFED PEPPERS

For some reason my brothers and sisters and I got it into our heads that stuffed peppers was the food that rich folks ate. When my mother got a load of that she decided to straighten us out. "Shoot, that's nothing but meatloaf stuffed in a pepper," she said, and set about creating this recipe. Now stuffed peppers are one of the most popular items at Sweetie Pie's and a family favorite. Even my son, Tim, can make them almost as well as me—almost. You can change up the meat, but don't leave out the saltines because they help hold the meat together. You can use a mix of beef and pork or even ground turkey if you want to keep it lighter. I like to use a variety of peppers to give the dish some extra color.

SERVES 4 TO 6

6 mixed bell peppers (green, orange, yellow, red)

1 ½ pounds lean ground beef

¼ cup onion soup mix, homemade (page 183) or store-bought

2 small onions, minced

2 small green bell peppers, cored, seeded, and minced

10 saltines, crushed

2 large eggs

1 tablespoon all-purpose flour

2 tablespoons sugar

1 teaspoon salt, plus more to taste

½ teaspoon ground black pepper, plus more to taste

4 cups tomato sauce

1. Preheat the oven to 400°F.

2. Slice the 6 colored bell peppers in half, cut out the membranes, and scrape out the seeds. Place the pepper halves in a large baking dish.

3. In a large bowl, use your hands to thoroughly mix the ground beef, onion soup mix, onions, minced bell peppers, and saltines. Add the eggs, flour, sugar, salt, and pepper and knead the mixture well.

4. Divide the meat mixture equally among the pepper halves and pat it in lightly.

5. Pour the tomato sauce into a small bowl, season with salt and pepper, and spoon half of it over the peppers.

6. Place in the oven and bake for 30 minutes, then spoon the remaining tomato sauce on top of and around the stuffed peppers. Bake for an additional 15 minutes, or until cooked through, basting with the tomato sauce mixture once as they cook. Serve immediately.

Mama and Daddy

My mama, Ora Gray, and my daddy, James Montgomery, were poor. My dad worked three jobs after he came home from serving his country in the army during World War II. They came to St. Louis from Mississippi when my dad got a job with the railroad.

On their wedding night my mom wore a nightgown her mom had made her and my dad wore pajamas made out of gunnysacks labeled NOT FOR SALE that his mom couldn't bleach out when she made them. He was so good-looking it didn't matter one bit.

We lived in a little house until we made it "big" and moved to the Pruitt-Igoe projects. Affordable housing started out as a nice place where folks who hoped to do better wanted to live.

My mama and daddy could make each other laugh and laugh, teasing each other about any old thing. I never saw them fight or saw their bedroom door closed. When I got older I wondered how the heck they made eight kids when that door was never closed. They didn't go to church, but they made sure us kids went every Sunday with our neighbor.

Everything in our house—in our world—revolved around Daddy. He worked and brought in the money and my mama stretched every dollar as far as she could to feed us all and keep us on the straight and narrow. Every two weeks I'd go in to work with my dad—if it was a weekend—and collect his paycheck to bring home to my mama. He'd put aside a little for himself and a quarter for each of us kids and then put me on the bus with the rest to take home to mama to manage the house. Daddy's friends nicknamed him "Money," and I sure don't know why because money was something he never had. Mama's friends called her Lil' Bit even though she had hips that spread from east to west. She was an original diva with a capital *D*.

Looking back, I realize my mom was a miracle worker, somehow stretching my dad's paycheck six ways to Sunday. She never had money for herself. If she wanted so much as some hand cream or a pair of nylons she'd say "I have to wait until James comes home." If we wanted a penny candy she'd say, "You have to wait until Daddy comes home."

Even without a lot to work with, my mama always kept a nice house, whether it was that first three-room shack with its outhouse or the four-bedroom apartment with a dining room, living room, and full bathroom. The furniture was well treated and everything was kept tidy—and we kids had our jobs to help keep it that way.

Being the oldest, I was always at one of their sides: Helping Mama in the kitchen or minding the younger kids or with my dad, making his famous cake with vanilla sauce (see the recipe on page 160), or going junkyard picking with him. I even would shave

Miss Robbie with her sisters, Linda and Janice.

my dad with his straight-edge metal razor.

In the summers they'd sit outside on the benches around the buildings with their friends, sipping on draft beer from a shared can. I remember itching for the day when I could be grown and sit around with them, talking grown-up talk. Once in a long while they'd go out for an evening together. On those rare occasions when my mom went out with her friends she'd bring home a couple of pieces of take-out fried chicken and wake us up to share it— just a bite each. My mom sharing a little bit of pleasure with us was heaven.

That's how it was in our house—we shared everything no matter how big or small: chores, treats, a little nibble of fried chicken. That was Mama and Daddy's rule. They didn't have to even say it—all for one, one for all, all the time—we got it.

SOULFUL SHEPHERD'S PIE

Shepherd's pie is one of those single dish meals that's good for a crowd. It's also economical and filling. Some folks use stew beef in their shepherd's pie, but I put ground beef in mine because it's less expensive. This dish is also a great way to use up leftover mashed potatoes. At the restaurant shepherd's pie appears on the menu as an occasional special, and it always gets sold out.

I put together my shepherd's pie sort of like lasagna—in layers—rather than the meat on the bottom and potatoes on top. I finish it off with a little shredded cheddar cheese on top, which isn't necessarily traditional, but it does make it bubbly and delicious.

SERVES 6 TO 8

Salt

½ cup baby carrots sliced into thin strips

2 teaspoons vegetable oil

1 small onion, minced

1 medium green bell pepper, cored, seeded, and minced

1 pound 80% lean ground beef or ground turkey

Pepper

1 tablespoon onion soup mix, homemade (page 183) or store-bought

3 cups Mashed Potatoes (page 112)

1½ cups shredded mild cheddar cheese

1. Preheat the oven to 350°F.

2. In a medium saucepan, bring 1½ cups of water with 1 teaspoon salt to a boil over high heat. Add the carrot strips, reduce the heat, and simmer for 6 to 7 minutes, until they are just tender, then drain.

3. Heat the oil in a large skillet over medium heat. Add the onion and bell pepper and sauté until the vegetables are beginning to soften, 2 to 3 minutes. Add the ground beef and mix it well to break up any chunks. Cook, stirring, until all the meat is browned, then season with salt and pepper and add the onion soup mix and cooked carrots.

4. Spread one quarter of the mashed potatoes on the bottom of a 9 x 13-inch baking dish and add one third of the meat mixture and one quarter of the cheese. Repeat the layering, finishing with potatoes on top and leaving a little cheese left over to sprinkle near the end.

5. Smooth the potatoes evenly over the top, place in the oven, and bake until the top is golden and crusty, 15 to 20 minutes. Sprinkle the remaining cheese over the potatoes and bake until the cheese is melted, bubbly, and beginning to brown. Serve in wedges like lasagna with a green salad alongside.

TAMALE PIE

The first time I saw a recipe for tamale pie was on the back of a box of cornmeal when I was living in California. Like I do with everything, I experimented with that recipe until I got it the way I wanted—with a little bit of southern soul. I spice my tamale pie with hot sauce. Some people like to put olives or capers in theirs; ½ cup pitted and chopped green olives or capers added after you remove the meat mixture from the heat should do it.

SERVES 6 TO 8

1 pound 80% lean ground beef
  or ground turkey
2 medium onions, minced
1 medium green bell pepper,
  cored, seeded, and finely
  chopped
1 cup tomato sauce
1 (14-ounce) can crushed
  tomatoes
1 cup water
2 teaspoons dark brown sugar
1 teaspoon ground cumin
1 teaspoon garlic powder
Salt and pepper
1 teaspoon hot sauce
1 cup shredded Colby cheese
1 cup shredded Monterey Jack
  cheese
½ recipe Skillet Cornbread
  batter (page 125)

1. Preheat the oven to 350°F.

2. Heat a large skillet over medium heat and add the ground beef. Cook, stirring to break up the pieces, until the beef browns, about 15 minutes. Add half of the onions and all of the bell pepper. Cook, stirring, for another 5 minutes, or until the onions and bell pepper soften.

3. Stir in the tomato sauce, crushed tomatoes, water, brown sugar, cumin, garlic powder, salt and pepper to taste, and hot sauce. Remove from the heat and set aside.

4. Spoon the ground meat mixture into a 9 x 13-inch baking dish and sprinkle the shredded cheeses on top, followed by the remaining onion. Evenly pour the cornbread batter over the top.

5. Place in the oven and bake for 35 to 40 minutes, until the cornbread is lightly browned and a toothpick inserted in the middle comes out clean. Serve cut into squares like lasagna with a green salad alongside.

SUNDAY ROAST BEEF

Growing up, we never had steak; Sunday roast beef after church was the closest we ever got to a nice thick T-bone, and to us it was like filet mignon. I use a roasting bag to make my roast beef for the most tender results, and putting the vegetables right in the roasting bag makes a one-pot meal. I cut my roast beef nice and thick, like steak, or thinly slice it for the makings for a great sandwich the next day.

SERVES 6

1 (3-pound) top-round beef
   roast

Salt and pepper

1 teaspoon all-purpose flour

4 tablespoons (½ stick)
   unsalted butter or
   margarine, sliced

4 cups Onion Soup (page 3),
   cooled

2 pounds baby red bliss
   potatoes

1 medium onion thinly sliced

2 stalks celery, chopped

3 carrots, chopped

1. Preheat the oven to 325°F.

2. Wash the roast under cold running water and pat it dry. Season it well with salt and pepper.

3. Dust a large roasting bag with the flour. Place the roast in the bag, arrange the butter pieces all over the top of the roast, and then pour in the onion soup.

4. Seal up the bag well and roast for 1 hour, then add the potatoes, onion, celery, and carrots and roast for another 30 minutes, or until a meat thermometer registers about 135°F for medium-rare. Allow roast to cool for 10 minutes and then slice into thin slices, not more than ¼ inch thick.

BACKUP SINGERS

vegetables, starches, and bread

You know, I never do like to think of these three as "side dishes." That makes it seem like they aren't as important as the main dish and if they weren't on the table they wouldn't be missed. Nothing could be further from the truth.

Growing up, we had a wide variety of vegetables, breads, and grains on the table. If times were tight, the vegetables came out of a can. We ate with the seasons; no one in Missouri expected to have a tomato in January. It wasn't until I got to California in 1961 did I experience the luxury of all kinds of fresh fruits and vegetables all year long.

Nowadays we expect to have a strawberry in February even if we live in Maine, and we can eat virtually anything from anywhere in the world. The thing is, I'm not so sure that's such a good thing. A big part of soul food cooking is about using what's at hand, including foods that someone had the good sense to put up while the getting was good in the summer. That was the original concept behind food in cans.

When I cook now, I always prefer fresh over a can or frozen. What I don't do is look for foods that are so far out of season that they just don't make sense on the table. Maybe that's because I naturally grew up eating "local" and "seasonal" before it was a fancy thing to do.

BLACK-EYED PEAS

Unlike a lot of other dried beans, black-eyed peas don't need to be soaked, but you should still pick them over for small stones and wash them in cold water. You can use any kind of smoked meat with your black-eyed peas, and a little okra added toward the end makes a thick broth. Cook them slowly or they'll become mealy and the skins can burst; using a slow cooker is an effective way of making them. Combine all the ingredients in a slow cooker and set it to low for 5 or 6 hours.

Serve as a side dish or with Hot Water Cornbread (page 121) as a one-pot meal.

4 strips bacon, cooked until crisp, 1 teaspoon of the grease reserved

½ pound smoked turkey, ham hock, smoked jowl, or diced ham

1 teaspoon ground black pepper

2 teaspoons onion soup mix, homemade (page 183) or store-bought

1 teaspoon sugar

1 small onion, chopped

2 cups dried black-eyed peas, picked over and rinsed

1 small tomato, chopped

1 cup trimmed, chopped okra (optional)

2 teaspoons salt

1. Place the bacon, smoked meat, pepper, onion soup mix, reserved bacon grease, and onion in a large saucepan and add 6 cups cold water. Place over high heat and bring to a boil, skimming any foam from the top of the pan.

2. Add the black-eyed peas, return to a boil, then reduce the heat to low and simmer for 30 minutes. Stir in the tomato and okra, if using, and continue to cook for 20 to 30 minutes more, until the beans are tender and the broth is thickened. Stir in the salt and serve.

PINTO BEANS

I make my pinto beans just like my black-eyed peas, but these beans have to be soaked because they're real hard. Soak them in cold water overnight at a ratio of 1 portion of beans to 3 portions of water. So, for 1 cup of beans use 3 cups of water, then drain the beans and cook them just like you would the black-eyed peas. You'll need an extra hour or so on the stovetop for pinto beans and an extra couple of hours if you are using a slow cooker but otherwise the recipe is just the same.

a trio of beans Beans are a staple in soul food cooking. First off, beans are easy to grow in most any type of soil, and they can be dried and kept all winter. Add a little ham or cured meat to enrich the flavor. Second, and most important, beans are full of protein and fiber—good nutrition for folks who worked hard but didn't have a whole lot to eat. These days beans are typically served as a side dish, but add some okra and you can turn a pot of beans into an all-in-one meal in no time.

LIMA BEANS

Lima beans are my favorite bean of all of them, and I especially like them with pork chops and mashed potatoes. If you are using frozen lima beans, follow the directions for making the black-eyed peas on page 78. If you're using dried lima beans (choose from the small or giant white variety), they'll need to be soaked in water to cover overnight before cooking and require an extra hour or so on the stovetop or an extra couple hours in the slow cooker.

Serve as a side dish to Stuffed Pork Chops (page 46) along with Mashed Potatoes (page 112).

SERVES 6

4 strips bacon, cooked until crisp, 1 teaspoon of the grease reserved

½ pound smoked turkey, ham hock, smoked jowl, or diced ham

1 teaspoon ground black pepper

2 teaspoons onion soup mix, homemade (page 183) or store-bought

1 teaspoon sugar

1 small onion, chopped

2 cups frozen lima beans, or 1¼ cups dried lima beans picked over and soaked overnight in 4 cups water

1 small tomato, chopped

1 cup trimmed, chopped okra (optional)

2 teaspoons salt

1. Place the bacon, smoked meat, pepper, onion soup mix, reserved bacon grease, and onion in a large saucepan and add 6 cups cold water. Place over high heat and bring to a boil, skimming any foam from the top of the pan.

2. Add the lima beans, return to a boil, then reduce the heat to low and simmer for 10 minutes for frozen and 30 minutes for dried. Stir in the tomato and okra, if using, and continue to cook for 15 to 20 minutes more for frozen and 30 to 40 minutes more for dried, until the beans are tender and the broth is thickened. Stir in the salt and serve.

BAKED BEANS

I like to make every dish my own—even ones that have been around forever, like baked beans. By adding ground meat, I've turned a simple dish into a heartier one, sort of like a sweet chili. Add a couple of pieces of cornbread and you've got a meal that will keep you nice and full for a good long time.

Serve with Roberta's Grandmother's Yeast Rolls (page 128) or Hot Water Cornbread (page 121).

SERVES 4 TO 6

1 tablespoon vegetable oil
1 green bell pepper, cored, seeded, and minced
1 onion, minced
1 pound lean ground beef or turkey
2 (15-ounce) cans baked beans
1½ cups ketchup
½ cup brown sugar
4 tablespoons (½ stick) unsalted butter, melted
Salt and pepper

1. Preheat the oven to 350°F.

2. Heat the oil in a large skillet over medium-high heat. Add the bell pepper and onion and cook for 2 to 3 minutes, until the vegetables are softened. Add the ground beef and cook for 10 to 12 minutes, stirring to break it up, until the meat is browned. Remove the meat from the pan using a slotted spoon to a large bowl.

3. Pour the baked beans in a large casserole dish and add the cooked beef mixture, ketchup, brown sugar, and butter. Bake for 20 minutes.

CREAMED PEAS

My mom always made creamed peas from canned peas, but I recently tried it with fresh garden peas, and it's even tastier. My mom's method of adding a little flour and water to thicken the milk goes pretty far back. It's like a quick version of what French chefs call a béchamel sauce, which is made from milk and flour, and you can use it to make a cream sauce for just about anything. Creamed peas are great with a Fried Chicken Dinner (page 193) or with a beef roast or baked chicken.

SERVES 4 TO 6

1 cup milk

1 tablespoon sugar

½ teaspoon salt

¼ teaspoon ground black
  pepper

4 tablespoons (½ stick)
  unsalted butter

2 cups fresh or frozen peas

1 tablespoon all-purpose flour

2 tablespoons water

1. Combine the milk, sugar, salt, and pepper in a large saucepan. Heat over medium-low heat to warm the milk, but watch it so it stays under a simmer. You do not want the milk to boil or it will separate. Whisk to dissolve the sugar, a minute or so.

2. Add the butter and let it melt, 3 to 4 minutes, then add the peas, reduce the heat to low, and cook for 15 to 20 minutes for fresh peas and 5 to 10 minutes for frozen. Remember, don't let that milk boil!

3. While the peas are cooking, in a small bowl, whisk the flour into the water to make slurry, making sure there are no lumps.

4. Test one of the peas—they should be soft but not totally mushy, and the fresh peas should still have a little pop when you bite into them. Add the flour mixture to the peas and gently stir. Raise the heat just slightly so the milk bubbles around the edges of the pan, and keep on stirring until the mixture thickens to a sauce consistency thick enough to coat the back of a spoon. Serve immediately.

GARLICKY GREEN BEANS

I created this dish as a way to enhance the taste of canned green beans, but fresh is generally my first choice nowadays. Ham or bacon and potatoes enrich the flavor and makes it more of a meal. I like to use butter, bacon grease, or chicken fat to cook up my onions and potatoes, but vegetable oil will do as well. In the Caribbean folks often add curry powder to their green beans, which you might try too—add about 2 teaspoons curry powder or to taste along with the rest of the seasonings. This is a good side to any roast or ham.

SERVES 4

4 tablespoons (½ stick) unsalted butter, bacon grease, rendered chicken fat, or vegetable oil

4 ounces chopped ham or Canadian bacon

3 small russet potatoes, peeled and cubed

2 tablespoons finely chopped onion

2 teaspoons minced fresh garlic

6 cups cut-up green beans (2-inch pieces), fresh, canned, or frozen

½ teaspoon red pepper flakes

¼ cup sugar

Salt and pepper

1½ cups water

5 tablespoons chicken stock

1. Melt or heat the fat in a medium saucepan over medium-low heat. Add the ham, potatoes, and onion and cook for about 15 minutes, stirring occasionally, until the potatoes start to soften. If you are using fresh green beans, add them to the pan now.

2. Stir in the red pepper flakes and sugar and season with salt and pepper.

3. Add the water, chicken stock, and green beans if you're using canned or frozen, increase the heat to high, bring to a simmer, then reduce the heat and simmer for 15 minutes, or until the potatoes are cooked through.

MIXED GREENS

Greens are another heritage black food, and while most people have heard of greens like collards or the newly stylish kale, the fact is there are many more greens to choose from. I use a bunch of different hard-leafed greens in my mixed greens because they'll all cook up around the same time. My favorite mix is turnip greens, mature spinach, and mustard greens, but you could use chard or beet greens. You can cook any one of the greens by themselves as well. Adjust your cooking time based on how tough the greens are. Collards will take the longest; I generally cook my collards on their own (see the recipe on page 88). I roll my greens up and slice through the short side of the roll in 1-inch segments so the pieces will keep some body but are not too big.

Just remember that greens like these take a long time to cook; put them on the stove first while you get the rest of the meal together. They reheat well, so you can set up a pot of greens whenever you have the time. They'll keep refrigerated for up to three days to add to whatever meal you are cooking. I like to serve my greens with Hot Water Cornbread (page 121) and Neck Bones Three Ways (page 50).

If you want to make this dish vegetarian, omit the smoked meat, use vegetable stock in place of water for more flavor and use 1 tablespoon onion powder instead of the onion soup mix. Add vegetable oil, and about 1 teaspoon smoked paprika to give them that nice smoky flavor. The bacon grease or oil added near the end makes the greens nice and shiny.

SERVES 6 TO 8

½ pound smoked turkey, ham hock, smoked jowl, or diced ham
2 large onions, chopped
1 teaspoon ground black pepper
2 tablespoons onion soup mix, homemade (page 183) or store-bought
1 bunch turnip greens
1 bunch mustard greens
1 pound spinach
1 medium turnip, peeled and diced
1 teaspoon sugar
1 teaspoon bacon grease or vegetable oil
Salt

1. Put the smoked turkey in a large pot with 8 cups water. Add the onions, black pepper, and onion soup mix, place over high heat, and bring to a boil. Lower the heat and simmer for 30 minutes, skimming off any foam from the top of the pot.

2. Meanwhile, use a sharp paring knife to cut the leaves off the stems of the greens and wash them well to remove any dirt or grit. Layer 3 or 4 leaves together and roll up them up like a cigar, then slice the roll along the short side into 1-inch pieces. Repeat until all the greens are cut up. Add them all to the pot along with the diced turnip and sugar.

3. Simmer for about 1 hour more, until very tender. Stir in the bacon grease and cook for an additional 10 minutes. Season with salt if needed, but the smoked meat may well be salty enough. Serve as a side dish with just about anything.

COLLARD GREENS

Like most soul food cooks, I don't mix collard greens with anything else—I cook them on their own. Collards have a strong, almost bitter taste that will take over anything they are cooked with. They take the longest of any green to cook, so plan accordingly—this is a good green to make ahead of time.

SERVES 6 TO 8

½ pound smoked turkey, ham hock, smoked jowl, or diced ham

2 large onions, chopped

1 teaspoon ground black pepper

1 teaspoon sugar

2 tablespoons onion soup mix, homemade (page 183) or store-bought

3 large bunches collard greens (about 2 pounds)

1 teaspoon bacon grease or vegetable oil

Salt

1. Put the smoked turkey in a large pot with 8 cups water. Add the onions, black pepper, sugar, and onion soup mix, place over high heat, and bring to a boil. Lower the heat and simmer for 30 minutes, skimming off any foam from the top of the pot.

2. Meanwhile, use a sharp paring knife to cut the leaves off the stems of the collard greens and wash them well to remove any dirt or grit. Layer 3 or 4 leaves together, roll up them up like a cigar, then slice the roll along the short side into 1-inch pieces. Repeat until all the greens are cut up. Chop up 1 cup of the most tender stems. Add them all to the pot.

3. Simmer the greens for about 1½ hours, until very tender. Stir in the bacon grease and cook for an additional 10 minutes. Season with salt if needed, but the smoked meat may well be salty enough. Serve as a side dish.

SMOTHERED CABBAGE, KALE, OR SPINACH

My favorite way of cooking cabbage is to smother it, and I smother spinach and kale too. When I cook spinach, I chop up a hard-boiled egg real fine to garnish the finished dish. For cabbage and kale, I garnish with chopped pecans. If you don't want to use bacon, try vegetable broth instead of the water, mixed with 1 teaspoon smoked paprika to give it a deeper flavor.

SERVES 6 TO 8

1 small head cabbage, halved, cored, 1 pound young kale, stems removed, or 1 pound baby spinach

4 ounces bacon, chopped

2 medium onions, thinly sliced

2 medium bell peppers, cored, seeded, and thinly sliced

1 teaspoon salt

1 teaspoon ground black pepper

1 teaspoon sugar

2 teaspoons onion soup mix, homemade (page 183) or store-bought

1 hard-boiled egg, minced, for garnishing spinach (optional)

¼ chopped pecans, for garnishing cabbage or kale (optional)

1. If using cabbage, separate the leaves, layer a few on top of each other, and roll them up like a cigar. Starting from the short end of the roll, cut the leaves into 1-inch strips; repeat until all the leaves are chopped. Roll and chop in the same way for kale and spinach; for spinach, don't remove the stems before rolling and chopping.

2. Heat a large, deep skillet over medium-high heat, add the bacon, and cook until crisp, 4 to 5 minutes, then use a slotted spoon to remove the pieces to a plate.

3. Add the onions and bell peppers to the skillet, reduce the heat to medium-low, and cook for 1 to 2 minutes, until the vegetables start to soften.

4. Add the chopped cabbage, kale, or spinach and add the salt, black pepper, sugar, and onion soup mix. Stir in the reserved bacon.

5. Add 3 cups of water, return to a simmer, then cover, reduce the heat to low, and cook for 30 minutes, or until the greens are nice and tender. Remove the cover and cook for 10 minutes more to evaporate some of the liquid. Serve, garnished with hard-boiled egg for spinach or pecans for cabbage or kale.

miss robbie says . . . put it on rewind Turkey bacon can be substituted for pork bacon; since it doesn't have much fat, you'll have to add an extra teaspoon of oil to the pot when you're cooking down the greens. Olive oil is a good heart-friendly choice, but vegetable oil is also fine.

BELL PEPPER QUARTET WITH ONIONS AND GARLIC

This is a simple, fresh-tasting recipe that goes with just about anything. I prefer to make it in the summer when peppers are in season as a light side dish. It's particularly good with Sunday Roast Beef (page 74) or Pork Roast (page 45). If you want to turn this into a salad, just let the peppers cool down and toss them with 2 teaspoons apple cider vinegar or balsamic vinegar.

SERVES 4

1 tablespoon olive or vegetable oil

1 medium sweet onion, such as Vidalia, thinly sliced

1 red bell pepper cored, seeded, and sliced ¼ inch thick

1 green bell pepper cored, seeded, and sliced ¼ inch thick

1 yellow bell pepper cored, seeded, and sliced ¼ inch thick

1 orange bell pepper cored, seeded, and sliced ¼ inch thick

2 cloves garlic, minced

Salt and pepper

Heat the oil in a large skillet over medium heat. Add the onion and bell peppers and cook until the onion begins to soften and the peppers start to brown, about 3 to 4 minutes. Add the garlic and cook for another 1 to 2 minutes, until you start to smell the garlic. Season with salt and pepper and serve hot, room-temperature, or cold.

FRIED GREEN TOMATOES

Fried green tomatoes are one of the best things about summer in the South. They are good to eat as a snack or a side dish, and I make a spicy dip to go with them. Now, there are two ways to make fried green tomatoes. You can dredge the tomatoes in a dry cornmeal mix or you can dip them in a batter made from cornmeal. I prefer to use batter so they get very well coated. The real traditional way is to fry these in bacon grease or lard, but the healthier way is to do it in vegetable oil.

SERVES 6 TO 8

TOMATOES

2 cups all-purpose flour

2 cups medium-grind cornmeal

2 teaspoons sugar

1 teaspoon salt, plus more for seasoning the tomatoes

1 teaspoon ground black pepper, plus more for seasoning the tomatoes

1¼ cups buttermilk

2 large eggs, beaten

2 pounds firm green tomatoes, cored and sliced crosswise ¼ inch thick

1 cup vegetable oil

DIPPING SAUCE

¾ cup mayonnaise

1 teaspoon mustard

½ teaspoon hot sauce, or to taste

1. In a large bowl, whisk together the flour, cornmeal, sugar, salt, and black pepper. Add the buttermilk and eggs and beat into a smooth batter.

2. Season the tomato slices with salt and pepper.

3. Heat the oil in a large skillet over medium heat. Dip the tomato slices in the batter, shaking off any excess. Lay the tomato slices in the oil in one layer—don't let them overlap or crowd each other. Fry for 2 to 3 minutes, until they are lightly browned on one side, then turn them over and fry them on the other side for another 2 to 3 minutes. Repeat until all the tomatoes are fried. As the tomatoes are fried, remove them from the skillet and set them on a plate lined with paper towels or a wire rack set over a baking sheet.

4. Mix up the dipping sauce by whisking together the mayonnaise, mustard, and hot sauce in a small bowl. Serve the fried green tomatoes hot with the dipping sauce alongside.

STEWED OKRA

Okra is a vegetable with a bad rap. Talk to most anyone from the South and they'll tell you they love it. Folks from most anywhere else will talk about how slimy it is. It's true that okra can be slimy, but that's only if you don't know how to cook it. First, the secret is to not chop off the tip of the stem—just cut off the tiniest bit of the dry part of where the stem attached to the plant. The second secret is not to boil it to the point where it breaks down. Young okra is tender and less slimy.

SERVES 4

2 cups water, chicken stock, or vegetable stock

2 tablespoons unsalted butter

Salt and pepper

1 teaspoon sugar

1 pound young okra, stem ends trimmed slightly

1 small onion, minced

½ cup peeled and chopped fresh or canned tomato

Bring the water to a boil in a medium saucepan over high heat. Add the butter, salt, pepper, and sugar. Lower the heat to medium and add the okra and onion. Return to a simmer and simmer for 20 minutes. Remove from the heat, mix in the tomato, and cover the pot. Let sit for 20 minutes, then serve.

FRIED OKRA

Fried okra is pretty much the same recipe as fried green tomatoes and, in fact, many people will fry the two together. Even though the okra is cut, the batter absorbs the "sliminess" when it's fried. You can eat fried okra as a hot snack as well as a side dish and you can use my hot dipping sauce (page 92) for them too.

SERVES 4

2 cups all-purpose flour

2 cups cornmeal

2 teaspoons sugar

1 teaspoon salt

1 teaspoon ground black
   pepper

1¼ cups buttermilk

2 large eggs, beaten

1 cup vegetable oil

2 pounds young okra, stem
   ends trimmed and cut
   crosswise into ½-inch pieces

1. In a large bowl, whisk together the flour, cornmeal, sugar, salt, and black pepper. Add the buttermilk and eggs and beat into a smooth batter.

2. Heat the oil in a large skillet over medium heat. Add the okra pieces to the batter and mix to coat. Use a slotted spoon to take them out of the batter and shake off any excess. Lay the okra slices in the oil in one layer—don't let them overlap or crowd each other. Fry for 2 to 3 minutes, until they are lightly browned on one side, then turn them over and fry on the other side for another 2 to 3 minutes. Repeat frying the okra in batches until all the okra is cooked.

3. Remove the fried okra from the pan and set it on a plate lined with paper towels or a wire rack set over a baking sheet. Serve the fried okra with ranch dressing or a jarred remoulade sauce, if you like.

miss robbie says . . . do a punch-in! This batter is also very nice for frying mushrooms; just follow the same instructions for frying the okra. Choose white button mushrooms that are no more than 1½ inches wide. Remove the stems and wipe the mushroom caps clean with a paper towel before mixing them into the batter.

SUCCOTASH

Succotash is another one of those dishes that makes me think of summer because corn is a main ingredient and in my day you only had corn in the hot summer months—not all the time like we do now. I like to put okra in my succotash, but you don't have to if you don't care for it. Another thing I do that's a little different is to add a touch of tomato sauce to give it a real good flavor.

SERVES 4

3 strips bacon, chopped

1 small onion, minced

1 green bell pepper, cored, seeded, and minced

1 cup frozen lima beans

2 cups fresh or frozen corn niblets (thawed and drained if frozen)

1 small tomato, cored and chopped

1 teaspoon sugar

1 teaspoon salt

1 teaspoon ground black pepper

½ cup tomato sauce

½ cup water or chicken stock

1 young okra, stem ends trimmed and sliced ¼ inch thick to equal 1 cup

1. Heat a medium saucepan over medium heat, add the bacon pieces, and cook until crisp, 3 to 4 minutes, then remove them from the pan with a slotted spoon to a plate.

2. Add the onion and bell pepper to the fat in the pan and cook until the vegetables begin to soften, 1 to 2 minutes. Lower heat to medium-low and stir in the lima beans, corn, tomato, sugar, salt, and pepper.

3. Add the tomato sauce and water, bring to a simmer, cover, and simmer for 15 minutes. Add the okra and simmer for 10 minutes more or until the okra is fork tender but not mushy. Remove from the heat, cover, and allow to sit for 10 minutes before serving.

CANDIED CARROT SOUFFLÉ

This is another one of those classic dishes you'll find in the South. You'll see it made up plain or sometimes with a pecan topping or even a cornflake topping. The key to a fluffy soufflé is lots of eggs and some baking powder. I whip up everything in the food processor or with a hand mixer to get it maximally smooth and fluffy.

Serve as a side to Baked Ham (page 44), Pork Roast (page 45), Roast Turkey (page 37), or Meatloaf (page 63).

SERVES 6

1 teaspoon salt

2 pounds carrots, cut into chunks

½ cup (1 stick) unsalted butter, softened

1 cup sugar

1 cup flour

2 teaspoons baking powder

1 teaspoon vanilla extract

¼ teaspoon ground cinnamon

¼ teaspoon ground nutmeg

4 large eggs, beaten

¼ cup evaporated milk

¾ cup flour

Small marshmallows for garnish (optional)

1. In a large saucepan, bring 4 cups of water with the salt to a boil. Add the carrots, lower the heat to medium-low, and simmer until tender, 20 to 25 minutes.

2. Meanwhile, preheat the oven to 350°F and butter or spray a 2-quart casserole dish.

3. Drain the carrots, cool slightly, then place them in a food processor (or, alternatively, in a mixing bowl using a hand mixer). Process until smooth, about 1 minute, stopping and scraping down the bowl as needed.

4. Add the butter and process until the mixture is smooth again, then add the sugar, baking powder, vanilla, cinnamon, and nutmeg and process until they are incorporated, about 30 seconds.

5. Add the eggs and evaporated milk and process for 1 to 2 minutes, until well combined. Stir in the flour and process until well combined, about 1 minute, then pour the mixture into the greased casserole dish and garnish with marshmallows, if using.

6. Place the soufflé in the oven and bake until it puffs up high and doesn't jiggle when you shake the pan, about 1 hour. Don't shake it too hard—you don't want the soufflé to fall! Serve immediately.

MASHED PUMPKIN
WITH BUTTER AND CINNAMON

I came up with this recipe while thinking about how pumpkin pie and sweet potato pie are so similar, with pumpkin pie basically a northern thing and sweet potato pie from the South. You can pretty much tell where a person is from just by asking what kind of pie they had on their Thanksgiving table!

With this in mind I thought it would interesting to experiment using pumpkin in a carrot soufflé or sweet potato casserole style dish, but without baking it, and after some trial and error, this butter-and-cinnamon-rich mashed pumpkin dish is what I came up with.

SERVES 4 TO 6

4 tablespoons (½ stick) unsalted butter
1 tablespoon vegetable oil
½ cup brown sugar
⅛ teaspoon nutmeg
2 teaspoons ground cinnamon
1½ teaspoons vanilla extract
2½ cups water
1 pound cheese pumpkin or pie pumpkin, peeled, cut in half, seeds removed, and cut into 1-inch chunks
¼ cup evaporated milk

1. Melt the butter in the oil in a medium saucepan over medium-low heat. Add the brown sugar, nutmeg, cinnamon, vanilla, and water, increase the heat, and bring to a boil.

2. Add the pumpkin, cover, reduce the heat to low, and cook for 30 minutes to 1 hour, until the pumpkin is soft and the liquid has thickened.

3. Carefully pour the mixture into a food processor, add the evaporated milk, and process until smooth. Alternatively, use a potato masher to mash your pumpkin. Serve immediately.

SUNDAY FRESH FRIED CORN

When I was growing up, I ate food that was in season, not because it was the "in" thing to do, but because that's just how it was. No one expected to get corn or strawberries in the wintertime. For us, dishes like fried corn were a treat because you couldn't get the corn but for a few weeks out of the year. I used to beg my mom to make this dish as much as possible when the corn came in, so I'd offer to shuck corn and cut the kernels off the cob if she'd fry it up. That was our arrangement.

Fried corn on its own is tasty; adding onion and bell pepper steps it up a notch. However you do it, it's important to keep stirring the corn mixture when it's in the skillet so that you get the most golden crusty goodness. It takes a little time, but it's worth it. My favorite way to eat fried corn is alongside Fried Green Tomatoes (page 92), but it's also wonderful with Fried Chicken (page 35), Meatloaf (page 63), and Mashed Potatoes (page 112).

SERVES 4

4 ears corn, shucked

½ small onion, chopped

1 small green bell pepper, cored, seeded, and chopped

½ teaspoon salt

½ teaspoon ground black pepper

2 teaspoons sugar

1 teaspoon all-purpose flour or cornstarch

3 tablespoons corn oil or bacon grease

1. Cut just enough from the bottom of each ear of corn so that you can hold it upright without it wobbling. Using a sharp knife, cut the kernels off the cob from top to bottom. Repeat with all the ears and put the kernels in a bowl. Using a spoon, gently scrape down the cobs to release some of the milk into the bowl. Add the onion and bell pepper and mix well.

2. In a small bowl, whisk together the salt, pepper, sugar, and flour and add it to the corn kernels. Mix well to coat the kernels.

3. Heat the oil in a large skillet over medium heat until very hot but not smoking, stir in the corn mixture, and cook for 1 to 2 minutes. Stir, and continue to stir every 1 to 2 minutes for 15 to 20 minutes, so that all of the corn gets a chance to get browned and crispy. Serve immediately.

ONIONY ROASTED CORN

This recipe is simple as can be, but you'll be surprised how good your corn is going to taste at those summertime barbecues. You can use canned onion soup—and I do in a pinch—but homemade always tastes better.

SERVES 4

4 ears corn, shucked
½ cup onion soup, homemade
   (page 3) or canned
Salt and pepper
Butter

1. Preheat a grill on high heat.

2. Place each corn cob on a piece of aluminum foil large enough to generously wrap around it. Pour a quarter of the onion soup over each corn cob and season with salt and pepper.

3. Wrap up the corn in the foil and place on the grill for 15 to 20 minutes, until the corn is tender. Serve hot slathered with butter.

ROASTED WINTER VEGETABLES WITH MAPLE GLAZE

I love to experiment, especially with new ways to work with the ingredients I usually use. For this recipe, I decided to combine those winter vegetables we most often use in soul food cooking and try to do something different and, also, a little healthier. This is a good side dish for heavier meats like Pork Roast (page 45) or even for Baked Chicken and Rice (page 32). I like things a little spicy so I use some cayenne in this dish but you can leave it out and it will be just as good.

SERVES 4

1 tablespoon vegetable or olive oil

1 large sweet potato, peeled and cut into 1-inch chunks

1 medium rutabaga, peeled and cut into 1-inch chunks

1 medium turnip, peeled and cut into 1-inch chunks

1 tablespoon No-Salt Seasoning Mix (page 182)

½ teaspoon cayenne pepper

2 tablespoons apple cider vinegar

¼ cup maple syrup

1 tablespoon chopped fresh chives

1. Preheat the oven to 400°F.

2. Pour the oil into a baking dish large enough for all the vegetables to fit in one layer.

3. Combine the vegetables in the baking dish and add the seasoning mix, and cayenne. Mix very well so the vegetables are well coated with oil and seasoning.

4. Bake for 30 to 40 minutes, until the vegetables are lightly browned and fork tender.

5. Remove from the oven, add the vinegar, stir well, then drizzle with the maple syrup. Garnish with the chives and serve.

ROASTED BRUSSELS SPROUTS WITH GARLIC AND BACON

This is another one of my experiments. I happen to really like Brussels sprouts, and everything tastes better with bacon. I added the garlic for extra flavor and sweetness, as garlic gets nice and sweet when it's roasted up. If you don't want to use bacon, add about 1 tablespoon of olive oil instead and garnish the finished dish with ¼ cup crushed pecans.

SERVES 4

5 strips bacon, chopped

1 pint Brussels sprouts, ends trimmed, sliced in half lengthwise

8 garlic cloves, peeled

1 teaspoon No-Salt Seasoning Mix (page 182)

1. Preheat the oven to 375°F.

2. Heat a skillet over medium-high heat, add the bacon, and cook until crispy, 4 to 5 minutes, then take them out with a slotted spoon and set them on a plate.

3. Pour the bacon grease into a 9 x 13-inch baking dish and add the Brussels sprouts and garlic. Sprinkle with the seasoning mix and mix well.

4. Bake until the Brussels sprouts are browned and crispy, about 30 minutes. Sprinkle with the bacon bits and serve.

BROCCOLI WITH RICE AND CHEESE

Rice casseroles are a quick way to do two sides dishes in one: your starch and your vegetable. This one in particular has become a classic southern recipe. You'll find that most versions call for frozen broccoli florets, and while that's fine, I like to use fresh whenever possible. Remember to wash your rice as I recommend on page 32 or you'll have a sticky mess.

Serve with Smothered Pork Chops (page 56), Sunday Roast Beef (page 74), or Pork Roast (page 45).

SERVES 6 TO 8

Salt

1 pound fresh or frozen
  broccoli florets

1 small onion, minced

1 cup long-grain rice (not
  parboiled or instant), washed

1½ cups Cream of Celery Soup
  (page 5)

4 tablespoons (½ stick)
  unsalted butter, cut into
  pieces

1 teaspoon onion soup mix,
  homemade (page 183) or
  store-bought

Pepper

1½ cups water or chicken
  stock

½ pound Better-Than-Velveeta
  Cheese Spread (page 180)
  or Velveeta cheese product,
  shredded

1. Preheat the oven to 400°F.

2. If you are using fresh broccoli florets, bring 6 cups of water with 1 teaspoon salt to a boil in a large saucepan over medium-high heat. Add the fresh broccoli and boil for 2 to 3 minutes. Drain and rinse with cold water. If you are using frozen broccoli, defrost it in a colander in the sink.

3. Combine the broccoli, rice, onion, cream of celery soup, butter pieces, onion soup mix, and salt and pepper to taste in a 9 x 13-inch casserole dish. Add the water and mix well. Stir in the shredded cheese and cover the baking dish with foil.

4. Place in the oven and bake for about 1 hour, removing the foil and stirring once about halfway through. Test to make sure rice is done. If it's not, cover and return to the oven for another 15 to 20 minutes.

MAC AND CHEESE

Macaroni and cheese is a classic southern dish and another one of those foods that everyone has a recipe for. I'm proud to say that mac and cheese is a specialty at Sweetie Pie's, and folks tell me that they come to the restaurant just to eat it, so we must be doing something right. The best mac and cheese uses a mix of different cheeses both tangy and mild. I make mine with evaporated milk, which gets it nice and creamy without becoming too thick or sticky. You can get your mac and cheese all ready up to the baking stage if you want to do it ahead of time—then you just pop it in the oven when dinnertime's approaching.

SERVES 4

1 tablespoon salt

2 cups small elbow macaroni

1 (12-ounce) can evaporated milk

2 large eggs

⅓ cup sour cream

4 tablespoons (½ stick) unsalted butter, cut into pieces

4 tablespoons margarine

⅓ pound shredded sharp cheddar cheese

⅓ pound shredded Colby Jack cheese

½ pound cubed Better-Than-Velveeta Cheese Spread (page 180)

¼ teaspoon ground black pepper

¼ teaspoon ground white pepper

1 tablespoon sugar

¼ cup whole milk

⅓ pound shredded mild cheddar cheese or American cheese for topping

1. Preheat the oven to 375°F and grease a 3-quart casserole dish with butter or cooking spray.

2. In a large saucepan, bring 6 cups of water to a boil and add the salt. Add the macaroni and cook according to package directions. Drain into a strainer and run cold water over it for a few minutes to cool.

3. In a medium bowl, beat together the evaporated milk, eggs, and sour cream.

4. Pour the cooled macaroni into the casserole dish and stir in the evaporated milk mixture.

5. Add the butter, margarine, sharp cheddar cheese, Colby cheese, cheese spread, sugar, black pepper, and white pepper. Slowly add the milk, stirring well as you pour. Pack down the mixture into a casserole dish and top it with the mild cheddar cheese.

6. Place in the oven and bake for 20 to 25 minutes, until the cheese is melted and lightly browned.

miss robbie says . . . put it on rewind! Lots of folks try to get a little extra fiber in their diet by eating whole grains. You can use whole-wheat macaroni in this dish just fine—make sure to cook it according to package directions, which will be a little longer than white-flour macaroni. Add a little extra milk too—about ¼ cup—because whole grains tend to absorb more liquid.

SOUL-STYLE SPAGHETTI WITH MEAT SAUCE

Basic spaghetti and meat sauce is a cheap and filling meal that can feed a crowd, so you can imagine that it was a go-to in my mother's kitchen. On special occasions I add shrimp to my spaghetti or sometimes even andouille sausage that I slice and fry up to add later. When times were hard, I'd just add some sliced hot dogs that I fried up. This is the kind of meal that can get dressed up or down based on what your pocketbook can afford.

SERVES 4 TO 6

1 teaspoon vegetable or olive oil

1 medium onion, minced

1 green bell pepper, cored, seeded, and finely chopped

1 pound 80% lean ground beef

1 teaspoon salt

½ teaspoon ground black pepper

Sugar

1 tablespoon onion soup mix, homemade (page 183) or store-bought

1 (16-ounce) can tomato paste

½ pound shelled and deveined medium shrimp (optional)

½ pound andouille sausage, sliced ½ inch thick (optional)

1 pound cooked spaghetti

1. Heat the oil in a large skillet over medium heat and add the onion and bell pepper. Cook until the vegetables start to soften, 2 to 3 minutes, then add the ground beef. Stir to break up the meat and cook for 5 to 7 minutes, until browned all over.

2. Pour off about half of the fat that comes out of the ground meat and stir in the salt, pepper, sugar to taste, and the onion soup mix. Add the tomato paste and stir well to coat the beef. Add 2 cups of water to the skillet, bring to a simmer, reduce the heat to medium-low, and simmer for about 10 minutes, until the sauce thickens up.

3. Add the shrimp and cook until the shrimp are just pink; remove from the heat.

4. If you are adding the sausage, cook it up while the sauce is simmering: Heat a medium skillet over medium heat, add the sausage, and cook until browned all over, about 7 to 8 minutes. Remove it from the skillet with a slotted spoon and add it to the meat sauce.

5. Combine the meat sauce with the cooked spaghetti and give it a good mix so all the pasta is coated. Serve immediately.

SMOTHERED POTATOES

Onions and slow cooking is what gives these potatoes their flavor. Unlike other smothering recipes, you don't need to use a roux or cream soup for a gravy; you just let the starch of the potatoes do the trick. The recipe is straightforward and simple, but boy does it taste good. Yukon gold or red bliss potatoes work best here because they hold their shape even after being cooked a long time.

Serve as a side to any roast or Stuffed Pork Chops (page 46).

SERVES 4

4 medium Yukon gold potatoes or 4 large red bliss potatoes
2 tablespoons unsalted butter
2 medium onions, thinly sliced
1 small green bell pepper, cored, seeded, and thinly sliced
1 tablespoon vegetable oil
Salt and pepper
Minced onion for garnish (optional)

1. Slice the potatoes in half lengthwise, then slice them again crosswise ½ inch thick into half-moon shapes. Place in a bowl of cool water to keep them from browning.

2. Melt the butter in a large skillet over medium heat. Add the onions and bell pepper and cook until golden brown, 4 to 5 minutes. Remove the onions with a slotted spoon to a plate.

3. Add the oil to the skillet, add the potato slices and cook until lightly browned, 2 to 3 minutes, then turn them over and cook until browned on the other side.

4. Return the onions to the pan and spread them on top of the potatoes. Season well with salt and pepper and add ¼ cup water. Cover the pan and reduce the heat to low.

5. Cook for 20 minutes, or until the potatoes are tender. Garnish with raw onions, if you like, and serve.

MASHED POTATOES

Mashed potatoes is another one of those dishes that everyone has their own way of doing. I put evaporated milk instead of fresh milk in mine—a trick I learned from my mother—which adds a little sweetness to the potatoes but also makes them creamy without becoming watery. My second trick is to use an electric mixer to whip the potatoes up to high fluffy peaks. I like to add just a little sour cream for some tang, but you don't have to add it if that's not to your taste.

SERVES 4

4 large russet potatoes, peeled
    and cubed
1 teaspoon salt
4 tablespoons (½ stick)
    unsalted butter
1 cup evaporated milk
2 tablespoons sour cream
    (optional)
Ground white or black pepper

1. Put the potatoes in a large saucepan with 4 cups of water and the salt. Bring to a boil over medium-high heat, then lower the heat to medium and simmer until the potatoes are fork tender, 20 to 25 minutes.

2. Drain the potatoes and return them to the pan. Add the butter and mash the potatoes using a fork or potato masher.

3. Place the pan over low heat and slowly add the evaporated milk, mixing it in with a handheld electric mixer on medium-low speed. Add the sour cream and continue to whip until the potatoes are fluffy and light, about 3 minutes. Season with pepper and serve.

POTATO PANCAKES

Potato pancakes are not something you'll find in soul food or southern cooking. I had heard about them for a long time, but when I finally tasted one, I didn't much like them, so I decided I'd do them one better. My version uses leftover mashed potatoes, onion, and egg. I like to eat these for breakfast with eggs, bacon, or sausage, but you can serve them as a starchy side dish for just about anything. They are also nice garnished with a little bit of shredded cheddar cheese or any other cheese you happen to like. Sprinkle the cheese on top right when they come out of the skillet so it will be sure to melt.

MAKES 8 PANCAKES

2 cups Mashed Potatoes
  (page 112)
1 small onion, finely minced
1 large egg
Salt and pepper
3 tablespoons all-purpose
  flour, plus more as needed
¼ cup vegetable oil

1. In a medium bowl, mix together the mashed potatoes, onion, and egg, season with salt and pepper, and beat to combine well.

2. Add the flour and mix until the mixture holds together firmly. If it doesn't, add more flour a little at a time until it does.

3. Form the mixture into 8 patties about ¼ inch thick.

4. Heat the oil in a large skillet over medium heat. When a pinch of flour tossed into the oil sizzles, then it's ready.

5. Carefully lay the patties in the oil, leaving ¼ to ½ inch of space around them—don't crowd them. Cook them in batches if necessary. Fry the potato pancakes until they are golden brown on one side, 4 to 5 minutes, then gently flip them over and brown the other side, another 4 to 5 minutes. Serve immediately.

CANDIED YAMS

Back in the day, when folks cooked yams they would put them on the hot coals left over from the cook fire. Most people had modern kitchens, of course, but we knew plenty of people who would use the embers from their fireplaces to make yams. I love that charred taste of the direct heat, so when I make my yams I put them right on the oven rack with a drip pan underneath them to catch the juices. Once they're cooked, I slice them open and put in lots of butter, cinnamon, and nutmeg, and it's delicious just like that—almost as if they'd been candied.

When I make candied yams in a baking dish, I use maple syrup or brown sugar like most cooks, but I like to use a lot more butter—enough so you can actually taste it.

SERVES 4

3 large yams (about 2 pounds), peeled and cut in half lengthwise

½ cup (1 stick) unsalted butter

4 tablespoons (½ stick) margarine

1⅓ cups brown or white sugar

¼ teaspoon ground nutmeg

1 teaspoon ground cinnamon

1 ½ teaspoons vanilla extract

2½ cups water

1. Cut each yam half into ¾-inch slices.

2. Melt the butter and margarine in a medium saucepan over medium heat. Add the sugar, nutmeg, cinnamon, vanilla, and water and bring the mixture to a boil.

3. Add the yams, return to a boil, then reduce the heat to low, cover, and cook for 45 minutes to 1 hour, until the yams are coated with a thick syrup and are tender but a little hard around the edges. Serve immediately.

MASHED RUTABAGA OR TURNIP

I think about rutabagas and turnips as the dish that separates when we were poor from when we got "rich." My mom made a big pot of them along with some Hot Water Cornbread (page 121) and greens (pages 87 to 90). It was filling food for when I was very young and we didn't have money. I don't think my youngest brothers and sisters even remember eating them because things had gotten better for us before they came along.

SERVES 4

2 cups peeled cubed rutabaga
   or turnip

4 ounces smoked ham,
   minced

1 small onion, chopped

1 teaspoon ground black
   pepper

⅛ teaspoon freshly grated
   nutmeg

1 tablespoon unsalted butter

1. Put the rutabaga in a large saucepan with 2½ cups water, the smoked ham, onion, and pepper. Bring to a simmer over medium heat and simmer until the rutabaga softens, about 30 minutes. Drain the water and reserve the meat and onions separate from the rutabaga.

2. Use a fork or potato masher to mash the rutabaga. Add the meat and onion back in, then add the nutmeg and butter and stir to melt the butter. Serve as a side to roast beef, baked or fried pork chops, or meatloaf.

SWEET POTATO CASSEROLE

This dish isn't that much different from my Candied Carrot Soufflé (page 99), but the sweet potato makes it a little heavier, and I top the dish with crushed pecans. Sweet potato casserole usually shows up at holiday meals like Thanksgiving or Christmas, but you can serve it with roast beef or roast chicken for a nice fall-season dinner too. I like to use a food processor for any dish with sweet potatoes so the final mash isn't stringy, which can happen if you mash them up by hand. Of course, the classic way to serve this dish is with mini marshmallows on top for a garnish, but cutting them out is a good way to keep your sugar down and the dish will still be delicious.

Serve as a side to Sunday Roast Beef (page 74) or Roast Turkey (page 37).

SERVES 4 TO 6

1 teaspoon salt

2 pounds sweet potatoes, peeled and cut into chunks

½ cup (1 stick) unsalted butter, softened

1 cup sugar

2 teaspoons baking powder

1 teaspoon vanilla extract

¼ teaspoon ground cinnamon

¼ teaspoon ground nutmeg

3 large eggs, beaten

½ cup finely chopped pecans

Mini marshmallows for garnish (optional)

1. In a large saucepan, bring 2 quarts water to a boil. Add the salt and sweet potatoes, lower the heat to medium-low, and simmer until the sweet potatoes are tender, 1 to 1½ hours.

2. Meanwhile, preheat the oven to 350°F and butter or spray a 2-quart casserole dish.

3. Drain the sweet potatoes and cool slightly. Place them in a food processor and process until smooth, scraping down the bowl as you need to.

4. Add the butter and sugar and process until the mixture is smooth again, then add the baking powder, vanilla, cinnamon, and nutmeg and process until incorporated, about 30 seconds.

5. Add the eggs and process for 1 to 2 minutes, until very well combined. Pour the mixture into the prepared casserole dish and sprinkle the top with the pecans and mini marshmallows, if using.

6. Place in the oven and bake until the casserole puffs up high and doesn't jiggle when you shake the pan, about 1 hour. The casserole will deflate a little as it cools. Serve immediately.

CORNBREAD DRESSING

Cornbread dressing is the best kind of dressing to have either stuffed in the turkey or on the side in a casserole. This recipe should make plenty for both. Remember, when you are stuffing a turkey, let the stuffing get cold before putting it in the cavity and don't pack it too tight. You can use a mix of green herbs like parsley and thyme in your stuffing, but I like to use poultry seasoning, sage, and my homemade onion soup mix. You'll see I use a combination of homemade and store-bought stuffing because the dry bagged stuffing is good for absorbing the liquid in the mixture so it doesn't get too soggy. The cornbread for the homemade stuffing should be a little stale so it's not too moist.

SERVES 8 TO 10

½ cup (1 stick) unsalted butter

1 small onion, finely minced

1 stalk celery, finely minced

1 green bell pepper, cored, seeded, and
   finely minced

1 recipe slightly stale Skillet
   Cornbread (page 125), crumbled

1 12-ounce bag or box cornbread
   stuffing mix

4 slices stale white bread, torn into pieces

4 cups chicken or vegetable stock

1 cup Cream of Celery Soup (page 5)

½ teaspoon dried sage

½ teaspoon celery seeds

1 tablespoon dried parsley flakes

1 tablespoon poultry seasoning

2 tablespoons onion soup mix, homemade
   (page 183) or store-bought

1 teaspoon salt

½ teaspoon ground black pepper

3 large eggs, beaten

¼ teaspoon baking powder

1. Preheat the oven to 350°F and butter or oil a 9 x 13-inch baking dish.

2. Melt the butter in a large deep saucepan over medium heat. Add the onion, celery, and bell pepper and cook until the vegetables are softened, 4 to 5 minutes.

3. Add the crumbled cornbread, the stuffing mix, and the torn-up white bread and mix well.

4. Add the chicken stock, cream of celery soup, sage, celery seeds, parsley flakes, and the seasoning packet from the dried stuffing mix if there is one. Mix in the poultry seasoning, onion soup mix, salt, and pepper. The mixture should be moist but not soggy.

5. Remove the stuffing mixture from the pan to a large bowl and cool completely.

6. In a large bowl, beat the eggs with the baking powder and mix them into the remainder of the stuffing.

7. Pour the stuffing mixture into the baking dish and bake until the top is golden brown, about 25 minutes.

HOT WATER CORNBREAD

Some folks might know this recipe as "hush puppies," and I hear down in Jamaica they add sugar to them and call them "festivals," but either way it's a must-have on a soul food table. The ingredients are simple, so the technique is even more important. My mama taught me that to make this recipe the water has to be real hot—basically at a rolling boil. The kind of oil you use makes a difference too. Nowadays I use a light oil like safflower, but we'd use bacon grease back then, and it sure tasted best. This cornbread is perfect with Mixed Greens (page 87).

1 tablespoon salt
1 tablespoon sugar
2 cups cornmeal
1 cup vegetable oil

1. In a medium saucepan, bring 1½ cups of water to a hard boil over high heat. Add the salt and sugar.

2. Slowly pour in the cornmeal a little at a time, mixing with a wooden spoon as your pour.

3. When all the cornmeal is added, continue to cook, beating it with the spoon to take out any lumps, until it is thick and smooth but not soupy and the consistency of thick grits, 3 to 4 minutes. Remove from the heat.

4. Heat a large skillet over high heat for 1 minute, then add the oil. Allow the oil to get good and hot—test it by dropping a little bit of the cornbread batter in it, and if it sizzles up right away, it's ready.

5. Form the batter into ovals about 3 inches long and ¼ inch thick. Lay them in the pan and fry for 2 to 3 minutes, until you see them start to get nice and golden, then gently flip them over and fry up the other side until it's golden too, another 2 to 3 minutes. Serve immediately.

miss robbie says . . . do a punch-in Because this recipe has but a few ingredients, you can make it your own by adding some scallions or a little chile pepper or whatever seasoning you like.

I sang my first song on stage when I was just ten years old, and after that I sang every chance I got: in the church choir, the school choir in community centers, and even under the streetlights with my friends. After I graduated school I started to sing in the local clubs with the group, and we joined up with a guy called Art Lassiter, who later became the father of my first son. He named us the Artettes, but life really changed when he introduced us to a husband and wife team called Ike and Lil'Anne, or Ike and Tina Turner as they became known later.

When we connected with Ike and Tina we started singing on a wider club circuit. Eventually they wanted a girl group to sing behind Art as the lead on a song they'd written called "Fool in Love." Well, when we got to the studio on recording day, Art hadn't shown, but Tina convinced Ike she could do the lead and we'd put on the background.

After the song was finished, we all went our different ways. The girls and I went back to singing around town and then later I went up to Chicago to be a female vocalist for Earl Hooker. On a visit home, I ran into Ike, and he told me that the song we had recorded was a hit. "A Fool In Love" became the song that put Tina and Ike on the map and the song that turned us from the Artettes to the Ikettes. It was 1960.

Having a hit song meant we had to go on the road. Our first stop was New York, where our record producer took us out to a fancy dinner. I think that was the first time in my life I ever sat down and ate in a restaurant with table service. I remember I had called my mom and asked her what to do. How I should act? Which fork or spoon should I use with each dish? She told me to just watch everyone else and do like them, and that's what I did. No one ever thought that was my first time in a fancy place.

After that, most of the meals we ate on the road were anything but fancy. We toured the South, and those were Jim Crow days. That meant segregation, and there weren't but a few black restaurants or integrated restaurants. One of the only

Miss Robbie, Gwen, and Stephanie singing background for Nancy Sinatra at Lake Tahoe. The outfits were designed by Bob Mackie, who later became famous for his designs and choreography.

Francis Hodges, Miss Robbie, and Sany Harrell as the Artette background singers, who later became the first Ikettes, performing the song "A Fool in Love."

places that would serve both black and white folks together was at the Greyhound bus stations, and if there was one in the town where we stopped, we made sure to eat there because we knew that we could get served a good hot meal.

Most of the time, though, we had to do the best we could. We ate a lot of sandwiches on the bus. I ate a lot of canned meat, and one of the other girls, Jesse, was partial to Vienna sausages. We all had to stock up on whatever we could buy in the grocery store and keep on the bus.

You can imagine that it didn't take me long to start to miss home cooking. I got a little hotplate and an electric skillet and went to work. When we rolled into a town and stayed in a motel, I'd cook for the whole band with my limited equipment. I would make cornbread, spaghetti, pork chops, fried chicken, fried potatoes, maca-roni and cheese, and fried rice. I even once managed to make a cake from a box mix. I did it just like I did the skillet cornbread by cooking it up on low heat, and when it rose, flipping it over on a plate and sliding it back on into the pan.

The best days were when we found a motel with a little kitchenette or a fur-nished apartment if we were going to stay awhile. Then we'd go all out making a full-on meal—fried chicken, roast beef, smoth-ered pork chops, a big pot of greens—you name it. Sometimes we'd even buy a cheap little hibachi and make us some barbecue.

But there were plenty of times when we didn't eat as good as we liked—either be-cause money was short, or time was short, or we just couldn't find a place that would give us a hot meal. It wasn't easy, but it made us strong and it made me a better cook. Trust me, if you can turn out soul food for twenty people on a hotplate and an electric skillet, then you *know* you're good.

SKILLET CORNBREAD

Everyone in the South makes buttermilk cornbread, and it's one of the foods I grew up on. Today a lot of people use a boxed mix, but this recipe is all I ever knew and we stuck to it in my family. People come to Sweetie Pie's and say "This cornbread is just like my grandmother's!" and that makes us feel real good. We use this mix a lot of different ways—you can put it in a muffin tin to make muffins, make it in an iron skillet, or make the dough stiffer and fry it up in spoonfuls for hoecakes.

When I was on the road with Tina Turner as an Ikette, I made this cornbread in a skillet over a hotplate in the motel room. I'd pour the batter in the hot skillet, cook it for a bit, put a plate on top of it, and then turn it over onto the plate. Then I'd slide that cornbread back into the skillet real gentle so the other side could finish browning up. Once it was done and you tasted a slice, boy, you could die!

SERVES 9

2 cups cornmeal
1 cup all-purpose flour
⅓ cup sugar
1 teaspoon salt
1½ teaspoons baking powder
2 large eggs
¾ cup buttermilk
½ cup milk
1 tablespoon unsalted butter
¼ cup vegetable oil

1. Preheat the oven to 350°F.
2. Sift the cornmeal, flour, sugar, salt, and baking powder into a large bowl.
3. In another large bowl, beat the eggs with the buttermilk and milk. Pour the cornmeal mixture into the egg mixture and beat it well so there are no lumps.
4. Put the butter and oil in a 9 x 13-inch baking pan and put the pan in the oven. Let that butter melt and start to bubble, then take the pan out. Shake it around a little to make sure the grease coats the bottom and sides.
5. Now pour your batter into the pan and put it back in the oven. Bake for 35 to 40 minutes, until the cornbread is firm on top, golden brown, and a cake tester stuck into the middle comes out clean.

BAKING POWDER BISCUITS

These biscuits are the first bread that I ever tried to make on my own. I was in sixth or seventh grade and I learned the recipe in home economics. Now, anyone from the South will tell you that big, fluffy, flaky baking powder biscuits are a dream on a plate, but they'll also tell you that not everyone can make them. My mom always allowed me to try my hand in the kitchen, so she let me go on ahead and make the biscuits at home—and when they were finished they were anything but dreamy. They came out tough and heavy, but my family ate them anyway so I wouldn't feel bad. From that day to now, I'm still perfecting my powder biscuits, and I've learned a few tricks on the way. First, your shortening or butter should be good and cold, and second, go easy on the dough—don't overknead it or it will be tough for sure. And I like to chill down the biscuits before I bake them, which assures a flaky finish.

MAKES ABOUT 1 DOZEN

4 cups all-purpose flour

¼ cup baking powder

2 teaspoons sugar

2 teaspoons salt

1 cup (2 sticks) cold
  shortening or unsalted
  butter, sliced

1½ cups cold milk or
  buttermilk

Heavy cream (optional)

1. Preheat the oven to 450°F and line a baking sheet with parchment paper.

2. In a large bowl, whisk together the flour, baking powder, sugar, and salt.

3. Add the shortening and toss well so that all the pieces are coated with flour. Then, using a fork, pastry cutter, or your fingers, cut in the shortening until the mixture looks crumbly with pea-size crumbs.

4. Slowly add the cold milk and gently mix the flour mixture until it just comes together. Knead once or twice so that the dough comes together well, but do not overknead it.

5. Lightly dust a clean work surface with flour and roll out the dough ½ inch thick. Cut out 12 biscuits with a 3-inch biscuit cutter. Bring back any of the dough trimmings, roll out again ½ inch thick, and cut out additional biscuits.

6. Lay the biscuits on the parchment with 1 inch around each of them. Chill the tray in the refrigerator for 20 minutes.

7. Brush each biscuit with heavy cream, if using (this will make the tops shiny). Bake the biscuits for 15 to 20 minutes, until they are fluffy and lightly browned. Serve with melted butter, maple syrup, jelly, or gravy.

ROBERTA'S GRANDMOTHER'S YEAST ROLLS

I got my heart set on making these rolls after having them at my neighbor Roberta's across the hall. Every Sunday before church she and her family had a big breakfast and there'd be smothered chicken, smothered potatoes, grits, and these yeast rolls that her grandmother made. Somehow I managed to get over there every Sunday at just the right time to get me some of them rolls. Eventually I got my hands on a recipe and tried them out until I got them just right—just like Roberta's grandmother's.

Over the years I realized that Roberta's grandmother's yeast roll dough was good for other recipes too, like cinnamon rolls, hot cross buns, or Danishes. I make Danishes the same way as I do my cinnamon rolls, but instead of cinnamon and sugar I sprinkle the rolled-out dough with raisins and chopped pecans or walnuts. For hamburger rolls, I brush the surface with egg white and add sesame seeds—a great bun for The Big Mo (page 64).

MAKES 12 ROLLS

1 (.25-ounce) package active
  dry yeast
¼ cup warm water (110°F)
3⅓ cups sifted all-purpose
  flour
1½ teaspoons salt
1 cup milk, scalded
¼ cup sugar
¼ cup shortening
1 large egg

1. In a small bowl, sprinkle the yeast over the water and put it aside until it gets bubbly. In a large bowl, whisk together the flour and salt.

2. In the bowl of a stand mixer mix the milk, sugar, and shortening and stir to melt the shortening. Let the mixture cool to lukewarm.

3. Add 1½ cups of the flour, then add the yeast mixture, the egg, and the rest of the flour. Using the dough hook or paddle attachment, beat this mixture on medium speed real well until it comes together and forms a smooth ball of dough. Put the dough ball in a lightly greased bowl and turn it over once so the whole dough ball is lightly greased. Cover with a clean dish towel and put it in a warm place to double up in size. Depending on how warm your kitchen is, that will be 1 to 2 hours.

4. When the dough is risen, pinch off pieces about the size of a tangerine and roll them like meatballs to make 12 rolls. Put them on a greased or parchment-lined baking sheet and let rise for another hour or so, until they double up in size.

5. Meanwhile, preheat the oven to 400°F.

6. Place the rolls in the oven and bake for 20 to 25 minutes, until they are golden brown and puffy. Serve hot from the oven or cooled to room temperature.

CINNAMON ROLLS WITH CREAM CHEESE FROSTING

My mom always used one recipe for multiple dishes because that's the only way to keep on cooking for a family of ten year after year. I learned that trick from her, like with this recipe, where I started with the basic yeast roll recipe to create these cinnamon rolls, danish, hamburger rolls.

MAKES 12 ROLLS

⅓ cup sugar

⅓ cup ground cinnamon

1 recipe Roberta's Grandmother's Yeast Rolls dough (page 128)

2 tablespoons unsalted butter, melted

FROSTING

2 (8-ounce) packages cream cheese, softened

4 tablespoons (½ stick) unsalted butter, softened

⅓ cup confectioners' sugar

1 teaspoon vanilla extract

1. To make the cinnamon rolls: In a small bowl, mix the sugar and cinnamon together and set aside.

2. Make the dough for the yeast rolls. After the dough rises for the first time, roll it out onto a floured work surface into a large rectangle about 18 inches long, 10 inches wide, and ¼ inch thick. Brush the dough with the melted butter and sprinkle the cinnamon mixture over the surface of the dough.

3. Roll up the dough from the long side and slice it into twelve 1-inch-wide slices.

4. Grease a 12-cup muffin tin and put each one of those slices into the holes. Let rise for 1 hour more, or until doubled up again.

5. Meanwhile, preheat the oven to 350°F.

6. Put the tin in the oven and bake for 20 to 25 minutes, until the rolls are puffed up and lightly golden. Remove to a wire rack and cool for 15 minutes before removing them from the tin.

7. While the rolls are baking, make the cream cheese frosting: In a large bowl, beat together the cream cheese, butter, confectioners' sugar, and vanilla until smooth. Frost the cooled cinnamon rolls with the frosting.

DANISHES

MAKES 12 ROLLS

2 tablespoons unsalted
  butter, melted
2 tablespoons corn syrup
1 recipe Roberta's
  Grandmother's Yeast Rolls
  dough (page 128)
⅓ cup chopped pecans or
  walnuts
¼ cup raisins (optional)
1 recipe Six Flavor Glaze
  (page 166)

1. Melt the butter with the corn syrup in a small saucepan over low heat.

2. Make the dough for the yeast rolls. After the dough rises for the first time, roll it out onto a floured work surface into a large rectangle about ¼ inch thick. Brush the rectangle with the butter and corn syrup mixture, then sprinkle the pecans and raisins, if using, on top.

3. Roll up the dough from the long side and slice it into 1-inch-wide slices to make 12 slices.

4. Grease a 12-cup muffin tin and put each one of those slices into the holes. Let rise for 1 hour more, or until doubled up again.

5. Meanwhile, preheat the oven to 350°F.

6. Place the tin in the oven and bake for 20 to 25 minutes, until the Danishes are puffed up and lightly golden. Remove to a wire rack and cool for 15 minutes before removing them from the tin.

7. Drizzle the warm rolls with the glaze and serve.

HAMBURGER ROLLS

MAKES 12 ROLLS

1 recipe Roberta's
  Grandmother's Yeast Rolls
  dough (page 128)
1 large egg white, well beaten
3 to 4 tablespoons sesame
  seeds

1. Make the dough for the yeast rolls. After the dough rises for the first time, pinch off pieces about the size of a tangerine and roll them like meatballs to make 12 rolls. Put each ball on a greased or parchment-lined baking sheet. Let rise again for another hour or so, until they double up in size.

2. Meanwhile, preheat the oven to 400°F.

3. Brush each roll with a little egg white and sprinkle evenly with sesame seeds. Bake the rolls for 20 to 25 minutes, until they are golden brown and puffy. Place on a wire rack and cool completely before using. The rolls will keep in a zip-top bag for up to 3 days.

HOT CROSS BUNS

Hot cross buns were a treat we always used to buy at Easter. You can make them ahead of time and freeze them before their second rising; defrost the rolls in the refrigerator overnight and they'll have risen enough to bake by morning.

MAKES 12

1 (.25-ounce) package active
dry yeast

¼ cup warm water (110°F)

3⅓ cups sifted all-purpose
flour

1½ teaspoons salt

1 teaspoon ground cinnamon

¼ teaspoon ground nutmeg

4 tablespoons (½ stick)
unsalted butter, cut into
small pieces

½ cup raisins

1 cup milk, scalded

½ cup sugar

1 teaspoon lemon extract

1 teaspoon orange extract

2 large eggs

1 large egg yolk

ICING

2 cups confectioners' sugar

1 teaspoon vanilla extract

2 tablespoons milk

1. In a small bowl, sprinkle the yeast over the water and set aside until it gets bubbly. In a large bowl, whisk together the flour, salt, cinnamon, and nutmeg.

2. Mix half of the flour mixture with the butter pieces, and using a pastry cutter or your fingers, mix together until the mixture is crumbly. Stir in the raisins.

3. In the bowl of a stand mixer, combine the milk and sugar and stir until the sugar dissolves, then cool to lukewarm. Stir in the lemon and orange extracts and add to the butter and flour mixture.

4. Add the eggs, egg yolk, and the rest of the flour mixture. Mix together real well on medium speed using the dough hook or paddle attachment, until it comes together and forms a smooth ball of dough. Put the dough in a lightly greased bowl and turn it over once so it's lightly greased all over. Cover with a clean dishtowel and put it in a warm place to double up in size. Depending on how warm your kitchen is, that will be 1 to 2 hours.

5. When the dough has risen, pinch off pieces about the size of a tangerine and roll them into balls to make 12 rolls. Put them on a greased or parchment-lined baking sheet and let rise for another hour or so, until they double up in size.

6. Meanwhile, preheat the oven to 400°F.

7. Place the rolls in the oven and bake for 20 to 25 minutes, until golden brown and puffy. Remove from the oven, place on a wire rack, and cool before icing.

8. To make the icing, in a small bowl mix all the icing ingredients into a smooth paste. Put the paste in a small pastry bag with a ¼-inch slit cut off the tip and make a large cross + with icing on the top of each bun.

THE BIG FINISH

desserts

Now we come to the part of the book that's going to be closest to any soul-food lover's heart: dessert.

As we know, soul food came mostly out of the South, and no one makes dessert like southerners. Sometimes I think we have more recipes for cake and pie and puddings and rolls and cookies and you name it than anything else.

When it comes to making dessert, I do not believe in skimping on the good stuff—the sugar and the fat. If you are going to make it, make it right or don't bother. But when you get ready to eat it—that's where the tradeoff comes. If you eat just a little, you can eat the real thing—and it will be more satisfying in the end.

I like to have a little something sweet on hand in case anyone drops by or if I'm going to stop in and visit someone myself. For this reason you'll find that I've indicated when a dessert can be frozen and kept on hand for those types of occasions.

You'll also notice that I love my extracts—vanilla, lemon, almond—you name it. I like to use a lot of them, but you can adjust the flavoring according to your particular taste.

BASIC PIECRUST

Nowadays it's easy to buy a frozen pie shell, but when I was young, if you wanted pie, you made the crust yourself. Still, a basic piecrust is something that every cook should know how to make. It's easy to do and easy to make extra and freeze it for when you want it. Piecrust made with butter tastes best, but one made with shortening is the most economical. If you use a shortening crust—like most of those from the supermarket—brush it with a little melted butter before you bake it off so it still has that buttery taste.

MAKES 2 (9-INCH)
PIECRUSTS

2½ cups all-purpose flour
1 teaspoon salt
1 cup (2 sticks) unsalted
   butter or shortening, cut
   into small cubes
¼ cup ice water, or more as
   needed

1. In a large bowl, whisk together the flour and salt.

2. Add the butter and, using a pastry cutter or fork, cut in the butter until the mixture is crumbly with pieces the size of peas. You can also do this in a food processor by mixing the flour, salt, and butter together and pulsing until you have that crumbly mixture with pea-size pieces.

3. Gradually add the ice water, mixing gently until you can form the dough into a ball. The ball should stick together but still be crumbly. Do not knead!

4. Cut the ball in half and wrap up each half in plastic. Now you have dough for two piecrusts.

5. Chill the crusts for an hour and then roll them out to fit your pie plate. Do this by flouring a work surface well and pressing the dough into a disk. Roll evenly in all directions, using a rolling pin, until you have a round crust that is 10 inches in diameter. This should be enough to fill the pie plate with a little overhang that you can tuck in or trim away after you fill the crust. You can also wrap and freeze the flattened balls of piecrust, or you can roll them out, then wrap and freeze them.

ROSALIE'S CHAMPION CHESS PIE

Making chess pie is sort of like playing a game of chess—there are winners and there are losers. The true champion is my friend Rosalie.

Rosalie started making pies for folks in her church by popular request—they were that good. She told me that once she delivered a chess pie to a friend who worked in a beauty salon and the folks there were so eager to eat it but didn't have a knife so they used the long end of a rat-tail comb to cut up the slices. Those beauty salon ladies ate that pie up so fast, and they asked if she had another and then another. Pretty soon she sold out all of the pies from her car at that one shop.

Rosalie's recipe calls for one teaspoon of vanilla, but I'm a fan of big flavor, so I typically use two or three, and I like to sprinkle finely ground pecans on the top for a little crunch.

MAKES 1 (9-INCH) PIE

½ recipe Basic Piecrust (page 136) 1 store-bought piecrust

½ cup (1 stick) plus 1 tablespoon unsalted butter, melted and cooled

3 large eggs

1½ cups sugar

⅓ cup milk

1 teaspoon white vinegar

1 tablespoon medium grind cornmeal

1 teaspoon vanilla extract

¼ cup finely ground pecans (optional)

Whipped cream for topping (optional)

1. Preheat the oven to 350°F.

2. Roll out the piecrust and lay it into a 9-inch pie plate. Do this by flouring a work surface well and pressing the dough into a disk. Roll evenly in all directions, using a rolling pin, until you have a round crust that is 10 inches in diameter. This should be enough to fill the pie plate with a little overhang that you can tuck in or trim away after you fill the crust. Brush 1 tablespoon of the melted butter onto the piecrust and prick the crust all over with a fork. Bake the shell for 10 minutes, or until the crust just begins to lightly brown. Remove the crust to a wire rack and cool completely. Leave the oven on.

3. In a large bowl using a fork, beat the eggs, then beat in the sugar, milk, vinegar, cornmeal, and vanilla. Beat in the remaining ½ cup butter until it is totally combined.

4. Pour the filling into the prebaked pie shell and, if you're using the pecans, sprinkle them evenly over it. Bake for 25 to 30 minutes, until the pie doesn't jiggle when shaken and a toothpick or tester stuck down the center of the pie comes out clean.

5. Cool completely and serve with whipped cream if you like.

miss robbie says . . . make it sing! I always brush my piecrusts with a little melted butter before I blind bake them—that way the shell is nice and crispy when you pour in your filling. It's also a good way to add some butter flavor to a shortening crust.

EGG CUSTARD PIE

Egg custard, basically a firm vanilla pudding, is pretty common in southern dessert recipes. It's the basis for chess pie, pecan pie, and coconut cream pie. Egg custard pie is the most simple of them all—a real something-from-nothing sort of recipe. But just because it's simple, don't think it isn't good—in fact, it's great. Like a lot of things in life, the more straightforward a recipe is, the better it's going to taste.

MAKES 1 (9-INCH) PIE

½ recipe Basic Piecrust (page 136) or 1 store-bought piecrust

4 tablespoons (½ stick) unsalted butter, melted and cooled

3 large eggs

1 large egg yolk

1 cup sugar

1 teaspoon white vinegar

1 teaspoon vanilla extract

2 teaspoons ground nutmeg

¼ teaspoon salt

2½ cups evaporated milk

Whipped cream for topping

1. Preheat the oven to 350°F.

2. Roll out the piecrust and lay it into a 9-inch pie plate. Do this by flouring a work surface well and pressing the dough into a disk. Roll evenly in all directions, using a rolling pin, until you have a round crust that is 10 inches in diameter. This should be enough to fill the pie plate with a little overhang that you can tuck in or trim away after you fill the crust. Brush 1 tablespoon of the melted butter onto the piecrust and prick the crust all over with a fork. Bake the shell for 10 minutes, or until the crust just begins to lightly brown. Remove the crust to a wire rack and cool completely. Leave the oven on.

3. In a large bowl, use a fork to beat the whole eggs and yolk, then beat in the sugar, vinegar, vanilla, nutmeg, and salt. Beat in the remaining cooled butter until it is totally combined.

4. Heat the evaporated milk in a medium saucepan over medium heat until it just starts to bubble around the edges. Using a ladle, slowly add the hot milk to the egg mixture, whisking quickly the whole time. Keep whisking until you've added all the milk.

5. Pour the filling into the prebaked pie shell and set it on a cookie sheet or baking sheet in case it overflows. Bake for 30 to 40 minutes, until the pie doesn't jiggle when you shake it lightly. The pie might puff up then collapse back down; that's OK. Cool completely and serve with whipped cream.

COCONUT CUSTARD PIE

There are some desserts that just make you think of the South, and coconut custard pie is definitely one of them. My version uses my basic egg custard pie recipe with a few tweaks, the most important one adding shredded coconut. You might also add 1 teaspoon coconut extract to give it even more of a coconut flavor.

MAKES 1 (9-INCH) PIE

½ recipe Basic Piecrust (page 136) or 1 store-bought piecrust

4 tablespoons (½ stick) unsalted butter, melted and cooled

3 large eggs

1 large egg yolk

1 cup sugar

1 teaspoon vanilla extract

1 teaspoon coconut extract (optional)

½ teaspoon ground nutmeg

¼ teaspoon salt

2 ½ cups evaporated milk

2 cups sweetened shredded coconut

Whipped cream for topping

Toasted coconut flakes for garnish

1. Preheat the oven to 350°F.

2. Roll out the piecrust and lay it into a 9-inch pie plate. Do this by flouring a work surface well and pressing the dough into a disk. Roll evenly in all directions, using a rolling pin, until you have a round crust that is 10 inches in diameter. This should be enough to fill the pie plate with a little overhang that you can tuck in or trim away after you fill the crust. Brush 1 tablespoon of the melted butter onto the piecrust and prick the crust all over with a fork. Bake the shell for 10 minutes, or until the crust just begins to lightly brown. Remove the crust to a wire rack and cool completely. Leave the oven on.

3. In a large bowl, use a fork to beat the whole eggs and yolk, then beat in the sugar, vanilla, coconut extract, if using, the nutmeg, and salt. Beat in the remaining cooled butter until it is totally combined.

4. Heat the evaporated milk in a medium saucepan over medium heat until it just starts to bubble around the edges. Using a ladle, slowly add the hot milk to the egg mixture, whisking quickly the whole time. Keep whisking until you've added all the milk.

5. Pulse the sweetened shredded coconut in a food processor so that the pieces are much smaller and resemble a coarse meal. Stir it into the egg mixture, then pour it into the prebaked pie shell and set it on a cookie sheet or baking sheet in case it overflows. Bake for 30 to 40 minutes, until the pie doesn't jiggle when you shake it lightly. The pie might puff up then collapse back down; that's OK. Cool completely and serve topped with whipped cream and garnished with toasted coconut.

PECAN PIE

Egg and sugar pies like pecan pie are classics in the South, and they make a lot out of few ingredients. Pecan pie is different in that pecans have always been expensive, so this is a dessert you'd really only see on holidays like Christmas or Thanksgiving or a special event. Pecan pie is made pretty much the same way as Chess Pie (page 138), but with the addition of pecans and a little corn syrup. I like to serve mine with some whipped cream on top, but vanilla ice cream is nice too. However you serve it, make sure it's totally cooled before you cut into it or you'll have a gooey mess on your hands.

MAKES 1 (9-INCH) PIE

½ recipe Basic Piecrust (page 136) or 1 store-bought piecrust
½ cup (1 stick) plus 1 tablespoon unsalted butter, melted and cooled
3 large eggs
1½ cups sugar
1 tablespoon light corn syrup
⅓ cup evaporated milk
1 teaspoon vanilla extract
1 tablespoon bourbon
1 cup chopped pecans
Whipped or vanilla cream for topping (optional)

1. Preheat the oven to 350°F.

2. Roll out the piecrust and lay it into a 9-inch pie plate. Do this by flouring a work surface well and pressing the dough into a disk. Roll evenly in all directions, using a rolling pin, until you have a round crust that is 10 inches in diameter. This should be enough to fill the pie plate with a little overhang that you can tuck in or trim away after you fill the crust. Brush 1 tablespoon of the melted butter onto the piecrust and prick the crust all over with a fork. Bake the shell for 10 minutes, or until the crust just begins to lightly brown. Remove the crust to a wire rack and cool completely. Leave the oven on.

3. In a large bowl, use a fork to beat the eggs, then beat in the sugar, corn syrup, evaporated milk, vanilla, and bourbon. Beat in the remaining cooled butter until it is totally combined.

4. Stir in the pecans and pour the filling into the prebaked pie shell. Bake for 25 to 30 minutes, until it doesn't jiggle when shaken and a knife stuck down the center of the pie comes out clean.

5. Cool completely and serve with whipped cream or vanilla ice cream.

KOOL-AID PIE

Kool-Aid pie is a rare treat to find nowadays, and if you do find it, it will likely be in the Deep South in states like Mississippi where my folks come from. The other popular recipe we make with Kool-Aid is Kool-Aid pickles, which may not sound tasty, but I'm here to tell you they sure are. For this pie, you can use any flavor Kool-Aid you like—grape is my favorite—and while the recipe calls for whipped topping, you can use real whipped cream just as easy.

MAKES 1 (9-INCH) PIE

10 graham crackers

10 vanilla wafers

1 teaspoon sugar

6 tablespoons unsalted butter, melted and cooled

1 envelope Kool-Aid drink mix of your choice

1 can sweetened condensed milk

1 (8-ounce) package cream cheese, softened

8 ounces whipped topping

1. Preheat the oven to 350°F.

2. Put the graham crackers, vanilla wafers, and sugar into a food processor and process into fine crumbs. Transfer to a bowl, add the melted butter, and mix it well—so that it looks like wet sand.

3. Press the graham cracker mixture evenly into a 9-inch pie plate and bake for 8 to 10 minutes, until firmed up but not browned. Remove from the oven to a wire rack and cool completely.

4. In a medium bowl, whisk together the Kool-Aid, sweetened condensed milk, and cream cheese until totally combined and smooth. Fold in the whipped topping, then pour the filling into the pie shell. Refrigerate for 1 to 2 hours to firm it up. Serve cold.

SKY-HIGH SWEET POTATO PIE

During all my years of eating sweet potato pie—and believe me, I've tried plenty—I never could understand why they were always so heavy. One day I decided to experiment and see what would happen if I added more eggs to puff it up and some baking powder for extra rise. What I got was a pie that ballooned up in the oven and that tasted nice and light when it settled down. My fail-proof formula is two eggs to one sweet potato and one egg "for the pie." I like a lot of flavor in my desserts, so my sweet potato pie has more cinnamon, nutmeg, and extracts than you might be used to, but trust me, when you taste this pie you will forget every other one you've ever had. Add some sweetened whipped cream to the top and you'll want to eat the whole pie in a single sitting.

MAKES 1 (9-INCH) PIE

½ recipe Basic Piecrust (page 136) or 1 store-bought piecrust

1 medium sweet potato

¾ teaspoon salt

½ cup (1 stick) unsalted butter or margarine, melted

½ cup sugar

½ teaspoon nutmeg

¾ teaspoon ground cinnamon

1 teaspoon vanilla extract

½ teaspoon lemon extract

½ teaspoon almond extract

⅓ cup evaporated milk

3 large eggs

2 tablespoons all-purpose flour

½ tablespoon baking powder

1. Preheat the oven to 350°F.

2. Roll out a piecrust. Do this by flouring a work surface well and pressing the dough into a disk. Roll evenly in all directions, using a rolling pin, until you have a round crust that is 10 inches in diameter. This should be enough to fill the pie plate with a little overhang that you can tuck in or trim away after you fill the crust.

3. Line a 9-inch pie plate with a piecrust and crimp the edges. Prick the bottom of the crust in a few places with a fork, then bake the shell for 15 minutes, or until it is lightly golden. Remove from the oven to a wire rack and cool completely. Turn off the oven.

4. Place the sweet potato in a medium saucepan with enough water to cover it and add ¼ teaspoon of the salt. Place over medium heat, bring to a simmer, and simmer until the sweet potato is fork tender, about 1½ hours. Drain and cool enough so it can to be easily handled. Peel and mash up the sweet potato. Measure out 1 cup (eat any extra).

5. Put the sweet potato in a large bowl and add the melted butter along with the sugar, nutmeg, cinnamon, and vanilla, lemon, and almond extracts.

6. Stir in the evaporated milk. Make sure the mixture is cooled completely, then add the eggs one at a time, beating well after you add each.

7. Stir in the flour, the remaining ½ teaspoon salt, and the baking powder and beat well. Pour the filling into the prebaked piecrust and refrigerate for 1 hour—this will allow the pie to puff higher when you bake it.

8. Meanwhile, preheat the oven to 350°F.

9. Bake the pie for 40 to 45 minutes, until the pie is firm when jiggled and lightly browned on top.

is it a sweet potato or is it a yam? If you are like my family, you probably call sweet potatoes yams and vice versa. I recently learned that while they were both brought here by our enslaved ancestors, they are not one and the same. Yams are in the lily and grass family, and they are starchier and drier. And that stringiness you sometimes get when you cook them up, *that's* the yam. Sweet potatoes are more watery and are actually related to morning glories! Who knew?

ICEBOX LEMON PIE

Icebox lemon pie was one of the hands-down favorites in my house growing up. If you've ever made key lime pie, then the way this pie is made will be familiar to you. When my mom made hers she used a straight graham cracker crust for the bottom of the pie dish and lined the sides of the dish with vanilla wafers. Each of us got a slice two wafers wide. As we got a little older, that slice of pie was a good bargaining chip. All of us kids had one day a week to wash dishes, but we had a system where we'd trade our slice of icebox lemon pie in return for doing someone else's dishes. My older brothers James and Harold always were willing to give up their slices so they could hit the road to hang outside that much sooner.

The custard of this pie is made with raw egg yolks, but they cook up nice and firm when you put the pie in the oven to brown the meringue topping. You'll also notice that there is a range in the amount of lemon juice—that's whether you want your pie to be less or more tangy. It's very important that you chill this pie in the refrigerator to get the custard to set just right.

MAKES 1 (9-INCH) PIE

½ cup graham cracker crumbs

5 tablespoons unsalted butter, melted and cooled

2 cans condensed milk

3 large eggs, separated

¼ to ⅓ cup freshly squeezed lemon juice

14 vanilla wafers

½ teaspoon cream of tartar

1 tablespoon sugar

⅛ teaspoon salt

1. Preheat the oven to 350°F.

2. In a medium bowl, mix the graham crackers and melted butter until the mixture looks like wet sand. Press the mixture evenly into the bottom of a 9-inch pie dish and bake for 10 to 15 minutes, until the crust is lightly browned and set. Remove from the oven to a wire rack and cool completely.

3. In a medium bowl, whisk the condensed milk and egg yolks until combined. Slowly stir in the lemon juice; the mixture will thicken like a loose pudding.

4. Place the vanilla wafers around the edge of the pie plate with the flat side of the wafers pressed against the edge. Immediately pour in the filling.

5. In the bowl of a stand mixer or in a metal bowl using a hand-held mixer, combine the egg whites, cream of tartar, sugar, and salt and whip until the mixture holds stiff peaks. Spread the meringue on top of the lemon pie and gently smooth it across to cover the surface of the filling.

6. Bake for 15 to 20 minutes, until the meringue begins to lightly brown. Remove to a wire rack and cool completely, then chill for at least 3 to 4 hours before eating.

miss robbie says . . . make it sing! When I was living in California and working as a session singer, I got to taste a lot of different vegetables and fruits including Meyer lemons. These lemons have skins the color of egg yolks, and they are a little sweeter and less sharp than regular lemons. When they're available, I recommend trying them in this pie.

CHOCOLATE CREAM PIE

MAKES 1 (9-INCH) PIE

½ recipe Basic Piecrust
(page 136) or 1 store-
bought piecrust
2 tablespoons cornstarch
2¾ cups evaporated milk
½ cup plus 2 teaspoons
sugar
⅛ teaspoon salt
6 large egg yolks, beaten
8 ounces bittersweet
chocolate
2 teaspoons unsweetened
cocoa powder
2 teaspoons vanilla extract
2 tablespoons cold unsalted
butter, sliced
1 cup heavy cream
Shaved bittersweet
chocolate for garnish

1. Preheat the oven to 350°F.

2. Roll out a piecrust. Do this by flouring a work surface well and pressing the dough into a disk. Roll evenly in all directions, using a rolling pin, until you have a round crust that is 10 inches in diameter. This should be enough to fill the pie plate with a little overhang that you can tuck in or trim away after you fill the crust.

3. Line a 9-inch pie plate with the piecrust and crimp the edges. Use a fork to prick the crust all over, then put a piece of parchment or foil over it and add about 2 cups pie weights or dried beans to weigh it down. Bake the crust for 10 minutes, then remove the pie weights and parchment and bake for 5 minutes more. Remove from the oven to a wire rack and cool completely.

4. In a small bowl, whisk the cornstarch in ¼ cup of the evaporated milk to combine. Set aside.

5. Pour the remaining 2½ cups evaporated milk into a medium saucepan. Add ½ cup of the sugar and the salt and heat over medium-low heat until it just starts to bubble around the edges of the pan, whisking well to melt the sugar, 3 to 4 minutes.

6. Have the egg yolks ready in a large bowl. Slowly drizzle hot milk into the eggs, whisking the whole time, until you've added about 1 cup of the milk. Add the mixture to the milk remaining in the pan, lower the heat to low, and whisk well.

7. Add the cornstarch slurry and keep whisking until the mixture starts to thicken up like pudding, 4 to 5 minutes, and it sticks to the whisk without sliding off when you lift the whisk out of the pan.

8. Take the custard off the heat, add the bittersweet chocolate and cocoa powder, and whisk until the chocolate is melted and well mixed. Whisk in the vanilla, then add the butter slices, whisking until they are melted and mixed in.

9. Pour the chocolate custard into the prepared pie shell and put it in the refrigerator to cool, at least 4 hours but preferably about 8.

10. In a large bowl, whip the heavy cream with the remaining 2 teaspoons of sugar until stiff peaks form. You can do this using a whisk, which will take about 3 minutes, or with an electric hand mixer or in a stand mixer, which will take 1 to 2 minutes.

11. Spread the whipped cream on top of the pie, smoothing it to cover the surface evenly. Garnish with the shaved chocolate. Keep refrigerated and serve cold.

FRIED FRUIT PIES

Fried pies are sort of like turnovers, except the crust is fried rather than baked and they're made with dried fruit rather than fresh. Some people use a regular piecrust or puff pastry to make these, but I think that gets too oily. Instead, I use a tougher dough that can stand up to the hot oil. This type of dough reminds me of the dough that East Africans make for their chapattis, a kind of flatbread they eat with most everything. I roll out my dough a little bigger than a tortilla so the pies are the perfect size to fit in your hand. You can dust the finished pies with a little powdered sugar, but go easy with it or you'll soon have more sugar on you than on the pie.

MAKES 12 PIES

FILLING

½ pound dried apples, peaches, or apricots, chopped

2 cups water

½ cup sugar

1 teaspoon ground cinnamon

1 teaspoon vanilla extract

1 tablespoon lemon juice

1 teaspoon cornstarch

DOUGH

2½ cups all-purpose flour

1 teaspoon salt

2 tablespoons sugar

1 teaspoon baking powder

1½ to 2 cups of ice water, as needed

3 tablespoons unsalted butter, melted

2 cups vegetable oil

Powdered sugar for dusting (optional)

1. Make the filling: Combine the dried fruit, water, and sugar in a medium saucepan. Place over high heat and bring to a boil. Reduce the heat to medium-low and simmer for 20 to 25 minutes for apples or peaches, 30 to 40 minutes for apricots. Take off the heat and let cool.

2. Using a large spoon or a potato masher, mash the fruit into a rough paste. Stir in the cinnamon, vanilla, lemon juice, and cornstarch and set aside.

3. Make the dough: In a large bowl, whisk together the flour, salt, sugar, and baking powder. Slowly start pouring in the ice water—just enough to bring the dough together into a moist ball without getting sticky. Start kneading the dough, adding a little more flour as needed to keep it smooth and elastic. Knead for about 15 minutes by hand or 6 to 8 minutes using a stand mixer fitted with the dough hook attachment—until it is elastic.

4. Knead in the melted butter and continue to knead the dough for 5 minutes more until its surface is smooth. Cover it with plastic wrap and let sit for 30 to 40 minutes or until, if pressed, it leaves a small indent that springs back slowly.

5. When the dough is good and rested, cut it into 12 equal pieces and roll them into balls. Flour a clean work surface and roll the dough into a circle slightly larger than a tortilla, about 10 inches.

6. Spoon a heaping tablespoon of the fruit mixture into the center of the dough circle and fold it over into a half moon. Use a fork to crimp the edges of the pie closed and set aside. Repeat until all the dough and filling has been used to make 12 pies.

7. Heat the oil in a large deep skillet over medium-high heat. Test to see if the oil is hot enough by dropping a pinch of flour into the oil; if it sizzles it's ready to fry the pies.

8. Working in batches, carefully lay the pies into the pan, making sure they don't overlap and aren't crowded—leave ¼ to ½ inch around each one.

9. Fry the pies until they are golden brown on one side and puff a little, 4 to 5 minutes. Gently turn them over and fry the other side, then remove to a baking sheet lined with paper towels or a wire rack set over a baking sheet. Repeat until all the pies are fried.

10. Lightly sprinkle the pies with powdered sugar if you like, and serve warm.

PEAR COBBLER

No matter what kind you love best, nothing says home to a Southern cook like a cobbler. At Sweetie Pie's, pear is the cobbler of choice, and I like to serve it with a nice scoop of ice cream. I'm giving you a recipe for poaching the pears from scratch because they have the nicest flavor, but canned pears will also do just fine. To make this pie fancier, you can lattice the crust: Roll out your top piecrust and cut it into 1-inch strips. Lay one set of strips across the pie about 1 inch apart, then layer the other set of strips crosswise over the first set, weaving the dough under and over the bottom layer like making a basket. Pinch the edges of the lattice crust to the edges of the bottom crust and brush with butter before baking.

MAKES 1 COBBLER

6 firm Bosc or Bartlett pears, peeled, stemmed, cored, and quartered

4 cups water

1½ cups plus 2 tablespoons sugar

1 cinnamon stick

1 tablespoon orange zest

1 recipe Basic Piecrust (page 136) or 2 store-bought piecrusts

3 tablespoons vanilla extract

1 tablespoon ground cinnamon

½ teaspoon nutmeg

1 tablespoon all-purpose flour

2 tablespoons unsalted butter, cut into pieces

2 tablespoons unsalted butter, melted

1. Preheat the oven to 350°F.

2. Place the pear quarters in a large pot with 4 cups of the water, 1 ½ cups of the sugar, the cinnamon stick, and orange zest. Cut a piece of parchment paper to fit the top of the pot and lay it gently on top of the pears—this will keep them from turning brown. Bring to a simmer over medium heat, then reduce the heat and simmer until the liquid becomes syrupy and the pears are fork tender, 8 to 10 minutes. Let the pears cool completely in the liquid, then cut them into ½-inch slices. Reserve the liquid. (If you want to use canned/jarred pears, just remove them from the liquid and slice them.)

3. If using homemade piecrusts: Roll each out into a square. Do this by flouring a work surface well and pressing the dough into a square. Roll evenly in all directions, using a rolling pin, until you have a round crust that is 10 inches square all around. This should be enough to fill the pie plate with a little overhang that you can tuck in or trim away after you fill the crust.

4. Line an 8 x 8-inch square baking pan with one of the piecrusts and add the pear chunks.

5. Add the ⅓ cup of the reserved poaching liquid or syrup from canned pears and the vanilla. Sprinkle the pears with 1 tablespoon of the sugar, ½ tablesoon of the cinnamon, and the nutmeg. Add the flour and dot the surface of the cobbler with the butter pieces.

6. Layer the second piecrust over the filling and pierce the crust in a few places to make vents. Brush the crust with the melted butter, then sprinkle it with the remaining cinnamon and sugar. Bake for 45 minutes, or until the crust is golden brown. Allow to cool and serve warm topped with vanilla ice cream or whipped cream.

miss robbie says . . . do a punch-in   Poached pears are nice to have on hand for a quick dessert, served on top of ice cream or with a sugar cookie. Follow the instructions for poaching the pears, but don't slice them; just let them cool and store them with their syrup in a jar in the fridge.

POUND CAKE

Making a good pound cake is, in my opinion, a skill every cook should have. Pound cake is delicious on its own, or you can dress it up with ice cream, fruit, chocolate sauce, vanilla sauce—just about anything. It freezes well too, making it a treat you can always have on hand just in case someone drops by. And you can add flavorings and mix-ins to your pound cake to create a whole new cake, like my Five Flavors Pound Cake.

MAKES 1 (8-INCH) CAKE

1 cup (2 sticks) unsalted butter or 1 (8-ounce) package cream cheese, softened

1 cup sugar

4 large eggs

2 teaspoons vanilla extract

2 cups all-purpose flour

½ teaspoon salt

½ teaspoon baking powder

½ cup sour cream

½ cup milk

1. Preheat the oven to 350°F and spray or grease an 8 x 3-inch round cake pan, tube pan, or Bundt pan.

2. Put the butter and sugar in the bowl of a stand mixer or in a large bowl using a hand mixer and mix on medium speed until they are creamed together, about 2 minutes. Add the eggs one by one, mixing after each addition until combined. Mix in the vanilla.

3. In a separate bowl, whisk together the flour, salt, and baking powder and add to the butter mixture in three parts, mixing well each time and scraping down the bowl as needed. Add the sour cream and mix to incorporate, then add the milk and mix again until well combined.

4. Pour the batter into the prepared cake pan and bake for 1 to 1½ hours, until a cake tester stuck right in the middle of the cake comes out clean. Let the cake cool 10 minutes in the pan before turning out onto a wire rack to cool completely before serving. Serve with fresh fruit or whipped cream.

miss robbie says . . . make it sing! I love to experiment with flavors to give my recipes that special Sweetie Pie's touch. One day I decided to add a whole bunch of different extracts to my pound cake recipe. In addition to the vanilla, I added ½ teaspoon each almond, lemon, orange, and rum extract, and my Five Flavor Cake was born. There are so many flavorings to experiment with from mint to coconut. I've even used 7-Up!

SCRIPTURE CAKE

My housekeeper Mary's mother was known for making this old-timey fruitcake that has a recipe that reads like a list of Bible verses. When Mary's mother died, the recipe was included in her obituary, and it piqued my interested. I did a little digging and found out that this is an old recipe that tests the baker's Bible knowledge, with each passage holding the clue to an ingredient. Back in the 1800s it was a way to teach girls both their baking and their Bible verses at the same time. The cake is also known as Old Testament Cake or Bible Cake. It's tasty with tea and makes a wonderful Christmas or Easter cake.

MAKES 1 (8-INCH) CAKE

2 cups all-purpose flour	1 Kings 4:22
2 teaspoons baking powder	Luke 13:21
1 teaspoon ground cinnamon	Kings 10:10
1 teaspoon ground mace	Kings 10:10
1 teaspoon ground cloves	Kings 10:10
½ teaspoon salt	Leviticus 2:13
½ cup (1 stick) unsalted butter, softened	Judges: 5:25
1½ cups sugar	Jeremiah 6:20
3 large eggs	Isaiah 10:14
1 cup finely chopped dried figs	1 Samuel 30:11
1 cup raisins	1 Samuel 30:11
½ cup almonds	Genesis 43:11
½ cup water	Genesis 43:24
1 tablespoon honey	Proverbs 24:13

1. Preheat the oven to 350°F. Grease or spray an 8 x 3-inch round cake pan or a Bundt pan.

2. In a large bowl, whisk together the flour, baking powder, cinnamon, mace, cloves, and salt.

3. In the bowl of a stand mixer or in a large bowl using a hand mixer, cream the butter and sugar until light and fluffy, 4 to 5 minutes. Add the eggs one at a time, mixing well after each addition.

4. Place the figs, raisins, almonds, and water in a food processor and process to a rough paste. Add the paste to the butter and egg mixture along with the honey and mix well to combine.

5. Add the flour mixture in two or three batches, mixing well after each addition and scraping down the sides of the bowl with a rubber spatula as needed. The dough will be stiff, like a loose cookie dough; you may add a tablespoon or two of water to make it easier to pour.

6. Pour the batter into the prepared cake pan and distribute it evenly, tapping the pan on the tabletop a few times to get out any air bubbles. Bake for 50 minutes to 1 hour, until the top is browned and a cake tester inserted into the middle of the cake comes out clean. Let the cake cool 10 minutes in the pan before turning out onto a wire rack to cool completely before serving.

miss robbie says . . . make it sing!

I like to put my personal touch on this cake by garnishing it with just a little bit of sugar and cinnamon sprinkled over the top. It makes the cake extra pretty, perfect for a holiday table.

DADDY'S SPECIAL-TREAT YELLOW CAKE

My dad, James Montgomery, didn't cook much, but he did have one specialty—yellow cake with vanilla cream sauce. We never knew when he was going to make it, which made it even more of a treat. Sometimes it would be on a weekend or even when he got home from work at the railroad—whenever the feeling took him to do it. He'd slice up the cake hot out of the oven, put it in a bowl, and then pour some of his luscious cream sauce on it. Dad used yellow cake mix for his, but it's even better when the cake is homemade. But don't be afraid to use a cake mix if you have to, it'll do just fine!

MAKES 1 (8-INCH) CAKE

2 cups cake flour

2 teaspoons baking powder

½ teaspoon salt

½ cup (1 stick) unsalted
  butter, softened

1 cup sugar

3 large eggs

2 teaspoons vanilla extract

¾ cup whole milk

Vanilla Cream Sauce (recipe
  follows)

1. Preheat the oven to 350°F and spray or grease an 8 x 3-inch round cake pan, tube cake pan, or Bundt Pan.

2. In a large bowl, whisk together the flour, baking powder, and salt.

3. Combine the butter and sugar in the bowl of a stand mixer or in a large bowl using a hand mixer and mix on medium speed until light and fluffy, 4 to 5 minutes. Add the eggs one by one, mixing after each addition until combined. Mix in the vanilla, followed by the whole milk.

4. Stir in the flour mixture in three parts, mixing well each time and scraping down the bowl as needed.

5. Pour the batter into the prepared pan and bake for 25 to 30 minutes, until the cake is golden brown and a cake tester stuck right into the middle of the cake comes out clean. Let the cake cool 10 minutes in the pan before turning out onto a wire rack to cool completely before serving. Serve with vanilla cream sauce poured over each slice.

VANILLA CREAM SAUCE

½ cup whole milk

½ cup heavy cream

¼ cup sugar

1 teaspoon vanilla extract

3 large egg yolks

1. In a medium saucepan, combine the milk, heavy cream, and sugar. Place over medium heat and heat, whisking until the sugar is melted and the cream just begins to bubble. Turn off the heat and stir in the vanilla.

2. Put the egg yolks in heatproof bowl and whisk well, slowly adding the cream mixture 1 tablespoon at a time. Keep adding cream and whisking until about ½ cup of the cream mixture is added.

3. Pour the egg yolk mixture back into the pan with the rest of the cream mixture and place the pan over low heat. Cook, whisking continuously, until the mixture thickens to a custard that can coat the back of a spoon. Do not let it boil!

4. Remove the custard from the heat and pour into a heatproof bowl. Cool to warm and serve over slices of yellow cake. You can cover any leftover custard by putting plastic wrap right against the surface and keeping it in the fridge, where it will last a couple of days.

miss robbie says . . . do a punch-in   The custard recipe doubles as a basic recipe for vanilla ice cream: Put plastic wrap right against the surface of the just-finished custard and refrigerate until cold, then churn in an ice cream maker following the manufacturer's directions.

ST. LOUIS GOOEY BUTTER CAKE

Next to St. Louis ribs and fried ravioli, gooey butter cake is probably the most famous food that comes out of my hometown. The way I've heard it, this cake came about when a worker at a local German bakery made a mistake while mixing up ingredients. Instead of throwing it out, they served it because it was the Depression and you didn't waste food. Now there are people who specialize in gooey butter cake.

A lot of folks take a shortcut and use boxed yellow cake mix, but I make mine from scratch. I like to add cream cheese to the "gooey" part to give a little tartness to this very sweet cake. Some folks go so far as to garnish the cake with confectioners' sugar, but I prefer fresh berries. And because it's so sweet, I serve it in itty-bitty thin slices. As long as you don't overdo it, you can eat nearly anything!

MAKES 1 (13 X 9-INCH)
SHEET CAKE

CAKE BATTER

¾ cup whole milk, warmed to
    110°F

1¾ teaspoons active dry yeast

2 cups all-purpose flour

2 teaspoons baking powder

½ teaspoon salt

½ cup (1 stick) unsalted
    butter, softened

1 cup sugar

3 large eggs

2 teaspoons vanilla extract

GOOEY MIX

1 (8-ounce) package cream
    cheese, softened

2 cups confectioners' sugar

1 tablespoon all-purpose flour

2 large eggs

1. First, make the cake batter: Put the warm milk in a small bowl and sprinkle the yeast over it. Set aside in a warm place until it gets frothy, 5 minutes or so.

2. In a large bowl, whisk together the flour, baking powder, and salt.

3. Combine the butter and sugar in the bowl of a stand mixer or in a large bowl using a hand mixer and mix on medium speed until light and fluffy, 4 to 5 minutes.

4. Add the eggs one by one, mixing after each addition, then mix in the vanilla. Mix in the milk and yeast mixture. Add the flour mixture in three parts, mixing well each time and scraping down the bowl as needed. Cover and set the dough aside in a warm place until it doubles in size, about 1 hour.

5. Preheat the oven to 350°F and spray or grease a 9 x 13-inch cake pan.

6. Now make your gooey mix: Combine the cream cheese, confectioners' sugar, and flour in a stand mixer or in a large bowl using a handheld mixer and mix on medium speed until light fluffy, 4 to 5 minutes. Add the eggs one by one, mixing after each addition. Add the vanilla and corn syrup and beat on high speed for about 1 minute.

2 teaspoons vanilla extract

1 tablespoon corn syrup

Confectioners' sugar or fresh
  berries for topping (optional)

7. Pour the cake batter into the prepared pan and use a spatula to spread it out evenly.

8. Spread the gooey mix across the batter and bake for about 45 minutes. You are going to see the cake puff in places, fall back down, and puff somewhere else—don't worry; this is normal. The cake is done when it's browned on top and firm, but a cake tester won't come out clean because of the goo!

9. Remove the cake from the oven and let the cake cool 10 minutes in the pan before serving. Because this cake is sticky it's best served from the pan. Serve dusted with more confectioners' sugar or topped with fresh berries if you like.

SIX FLAVOR GLAZE

This is a good quick glaze for a pound cake, Danish, or any simple cake that needs a little pizzazz. It's based on a standard southern cake glaze, but I love flavor so I add a whole bunch of flavoring extracts to make it sing!

MAKES ½ CUP

½ cup sugar

¼ cup water

½ teaspoon coconut extract

½ teaspoon rum extract

½ teaspoon lemon extract

½ teaspoon vanilla extract

½ teaspoon almond extract

½ teaspoon butter extract

1. Combine all the ingredients in a small saucepan, bring to boil over medium heat, and cook until it's thick enough to coat the back of a spoon without dripping.

2. Pour or drizzle on your cake while the sauce is still warm.

CARAMEL CAKE

This is a basic yellow cake with a mouthwatering, gooey caramel frosting. I like to make this in a Bundt cake form and drizzle the caramel on top, letting it drip down the sides. The plating is gorgeous, perfect for a special occasion. Sometimes I like to make the cake in three layers and drizzle the caramel between each layer and over the top of the cake.

MAKES 1 BUNDT CAKE

CAKE

2 cups cake flour

2 teaspoons baking powder

½ teaspoon salt

½ cup (1 stick) unsalted
  butter, softened

1 cup sugar

3 large eggs

2 teaspoons vanilla extract

¾ cup whole milk

CARAMEL FROSTING

¾ cup (1½ sticks) butter

3 cups sugar

1 12-ounce can evaporated
  milk

1 tablespoon vanilla extract

1. Preheat the oven to 350°F and spray or grease a Bundt pan.

2. Make the cake: In a large bowl, whisk together the flour, baking powder, and salt.

3. Combine the butter and sugar together in the bowl of a stand mixer or in a large bowl using a hand mixer and mix on medium speed until light and fluffy, 4 to 5 minutes.

4. Add the eggs one by one, mixing to combine after each addition. Mix in the vanilla, then the milk. Add the flour mixture in three parts, mixing well after each addition and scraping down the bowl as needed.

5. Pour the batter into the prepared pan and bake for 30 to 40 minutes, until the cake is golden brown and a cake tester stuck right into the middle of the cake comes out clean. Let the cake cool 10 minutes in the pan before turning out onto a wire rack to cool completely before serving.

6. While the cake is baking, make the caramel sauce: Melt the butter in a large skillet over low heat. Add the sugar and use a wooden spoon to stir it well and cook, stirring continuously, until the sugar is melted, the mixture is golden brown, and it reaches the caramel stage, 350°F on a candy thermometer. Another way to test it is to let a small amount drip off the spoon into a cup of cold water. When it gets hard enough to crack between your fingers when you pull it out, it's ready.

7. Slowly pour in the evaporated milk and stir to combine. Slowly add the vanilla and keep stirring until the caramel gets to about 240°F on a candy thermometer, or when you drop a small amount into a cup of cold water it comes together into a ball but when you pull it out you can still smash it between your fingers.

8. Pour the caramel sauce all around the cake and let it drop down the sides inside and out.

PINEAPPLE UPSIDE-DOWN CAKE

Pineapple upside-down cake is best made in a skillet—that's the traditional way—although many people do make it in a regular cake pan in the oven from start to finish. This cake uses my basic yellow cake as a base, another reason why you'll never go wrong putting in the effort to getting good at making a basic homemade yellow cake. Pineapple upside-down cake is the kind of dessert I make at home instead of at the restaurant because it takes some care to get the caramel just right and it's best eaten almost as soon as it's made.

MAKES 1 (9-INCH) CAKE

CAKE

2 cups cake flour

2 teaspoons baking powder

½ teaspoon salt

½ cup (1 stick) unsalted
   butter, softened

1 cup sugar

3 large eggs

2 teaspoons vanilla extract

¾ cup whole milk

PINEAPPLE BASE

½ cup (1 stick) unsalted butter

1 cup brown sugar

1 (8-ounce) can pineapple
   rings

Stemmed maraschino cherries

1. Preheat the oven to 350°F.

2. Make the cake: In a large bowl, whisk together the flour, baking powder, and salt.

3. Combine the butter and sugar in the bowl of a stand mixer or in a large bowl using a hand mixer and mix on medium speed until light and fluffy, 4 to 5 minutes. Add the eggs one by one, mixing after each addition. Mix in the vanilla, then the milk.

4. Stir in the flour mixture in three parts, mixing well after each addition and scraping down the bowl as needed.

5. Make the pineapple base: Melt the butter in a large skillet over low heat and add the sugar. Cook, stirring constantly, until the sugar melts, 1 to 2 minutes, being very careful that it does not scorch. Layer the pineapple rings in one layer in the sugar mixture and put a maraschino cherry inside each pineapple ring.

6. Pour the cake batter over the pineapple mixture and smooth the top. Put the skillet in the oven and bake for 25 to 30 minutes, until the cake rises and a tester inserted in the middle comes out clean.

7. Remove the skillet from the oven and let it cool enough so it can be handled. Place a large plate over the skillet and flip it over in a smooth, quick motion so the bottom of the cake becomes the top. Serve slightly warm.

singing for my supper

When the Ikettes decided to head out on our own, we changed our name and hit the road as the Mirettes. We made the usual rounds—did the chitlin' circuit and had a couple of mediocre hits. The group broke up when Venetta, one of the original girls, left the group.

We lived in Los Angeles, and even went to Europe on tour, where Venetta hooked us up as background singers. We sang for everyone: Quincy Jones, Barbra Streisand, Stevie Wonder, Nancy Sinatra, and even white rock bands. A lot of times a musician

Miss Robbie singing lead in her own band, called Special Kind, at Sanford's Supper Club in St. Louis, Missouri.

Miss Robbie at the Desert Inn, singing background for Nancy Sinatra in Las Vegas.

you might know as the country singer Glen Campbell would play the guitar.

You might notice I say we sang "for" everyone—that's because we often didn't see the folks who we were backing up. We'd come in and lay the tracks down long after they had left the studio. Sometimes we'd hear a song come on the radio and say "damn that sure sounds like us!" and we'd find out that it was.

We even did TV work—singing jingles and backgrounds for programs including *The Sonny and Cher Comedy Hour,* Dick Clark's *American Bandstand, Shindig!,* and *The Midnight Special.*

In 1972, a girlfriend from New Orleans, Tammy Lynn, couldn't do background for the singer she was touring with anymore, and she asked me to fill in. That's how I got hooked up with Dr. John—and that was a good steady gig for eight years in between background gigs.

In a lot of ways I was living a performer's dream—I was actually working and making a good living as a singer, and there's not a lot who can say that. Even when I first started to have troubles with what would be later diagnosed as sarcoidosis, which led to hospitalization and lung collapses, I kept on singing. When I wasn't singing, I was doing the other thing I do best: cooking.

Those were great times, cooking and having all the folks I worked with come over to eat. There were musicians, singers, producers, agents—everyone. Luckily, soul food cooking is made for a crowd and on a budget, so it was easy enough to treat everyone to my wings, greens, cornbread, ribs, and lots and lots of desserts. One of the easiest deserts to make for a crowd is bread pudding—and it's a great way to use up stale bread, which I usually had a lot of traveling around as much as I did. And aside from the butter, it's an inexpensive dessert.

Jenae (Timmy's mom), Janice (Miss Robbie's sister), and Miss Robbie at the NAACP Image 2015 Awards Ceremony in Los Angeles.

BREAD PUDDING

My mama used to call bread pudding "poor man's dessert" because it was a way to use up stale bread and items you usually had around like canned milk and some sugar and eggs to turn it into something sweet and delicious. I dress my bread pudding up with a pineapple custard sauce and I happen to like a lot of raisins in the pudding itself. If you don't like raisins, you can leave them out.

SERVES 6 TO 8

PUDDING

6 cups stale bread or rolls cut into ½-inch cubes
2 cans evaporated milk
1 cup (2 sticks) unsalted butter, melted and cooled
2 cups sugar
1 teaspoon nutmeg
1 teaspoon ground cinnamon
4 large eggs, beaten
1 teaspoon vanilla extract
1 teaspoon lemon extract
¾ cup raisins

PINEAPPLE CREAM SAUCE

1 cup crushed unsweetened pineapple
1 tablespoon unsalted butter, melted
1 recipe Vanilla Cream Sauce (page 161)

1. Preheat the oven to 350°F and grease a 3-quart casserole dish.

2. Put the bread pieces in a large bowl with the evaporated milk and butter. Mix very well to moisten the bread. Add the sugar, nutmeg, cinnamon, and eggs and keep mixing until it becomes mush. Add the vanilla and lemon extracts and then the raisins.

3. Pour the bread mixture into the greased casserole dish and bake for 20 to 30 minutes, until the top is firm and lightly golden. Remove from the oven and let cool slightly.

4. While the bread pudding is baking, make the sauce: Add the crushed pineapple and butter to the cream sauce and mix it well.

5. Slice the bread pudding and serve, with 2 to 3 tablespoons of the pineapple cream sauce spooned over each slice.

PEANUT OR PECAN BRITTLE

My grandmother Miss Ozela was famous for her tea cakes, but she was also known for her nut brittle. She kept it in a tin and she'd dole it out to us kids as a treat. Put some into little candy bags and tie them up with a pretty ribbon to make a great gift. Add my cranberry sauce (page 178) and a small jar of my homemade onion soup (page 183) and you've got a nice personalized holiday gift basket.

MAKES 1 POUND

½ cup (1 stick) unsalted butter
1 teaspoon vanilla extract
2 cups sugar
⅛ teaspoon salt
2 cups peanuts or pecan pieces

1. Melt the butter in a large skillet over low heat. Add the sugar and vanilla and use a wooden spoon to stir it well.

2. Keep on cooking the butter and sugar, mixing the whole time, until the sugar melts into the butter, the mixture is golden brown, and it reaches the caramel stage, 350°F on a candy thermometer. Another way to test it is to let a small amount drip off the spoon into a cup of cold water. If it gets hard enough to crack between your fingers when you pull it out, then it's ready.

3. Stir in the peanuts and spread the mixture on a lightly greased cookie sheet. Set aside to harden completely, at least 1 hour, then break it up into pieces. Store in airtight container.

MISS OZELA'S OLD-FASHIONED SOUTHERN TEA CAKES

My grandmother Ozela Montgomery lived in Starkville, Mississippi, and after we moved to St. Louis when I was ten years old we mostly saw her on holidays or special occasions. We called her Miss Ozela, and I remember that she always wore long dresses to hide the fact that she had lost a leg to infection from a foot wound when she was younger. From the way she got around, you'd never know she had a disability. She even taught all us kids to walk from the time we were toddlers by telling us to hang on to the long braid she wore down her back and to go on and walk after her.

Miss Ozela didn't have much money, but whenever we were coming to visit there was always one of two treats: a piece of Bazooka bubble gum that she'd buy by the case or a home-made tea cake, which she stored in an old lard can she kept under her bed.

Tea cakes are basically a sugar cookie, and some folks make a version with sour cream mixed in to make it special, but Miss Ozela always stuck to the basic recipe. When I make mine I roll them out real thin because that's how I like them, but you can make them a little thicker if you like. Miss Ozela always used a cup or glass as a cookie cutter, but a regular cookie cutter or biscuit cutter will do just fine.

MAKES ABOUT 6 DOZEN

½ cup (1 stick) unsalted
  butter, softened
½ cup sugar
2 large eggs
2 teaspoons vanilla extract
1 teaspoon lemon extract
3½ cups self-rising flour, plus
  extra for rolling
1 teaspoon ground nutmeg

1. Preheat the oven to 350°F and grease 2 cookie sheets.

2. Combine the butter and sugar in the bowl of a stand mixer or in a large bowl using hand mixer on medium and mix together until fluffy, about 4 minutes. Add the eggs one at a time, mixing well after each addition. Add the vanilla and lemon extracts and mix well.

3. In a separate large bowl, whisk the flour and nutmeg together, and mix it into the butter mixture to make a stiff but soft dough.

4. Dust a work surface well with the flour; dust the dough with flour too. Roll out the dough to about ⅛ inch thick and use a 3-inch cookie cutter to cut out cookies.

5. Put the cookies on the prepared cookie sheets (you'll need to make them in batches) and bake until firm and just lightly browned, 10 to 12 minutes. Remove from the oven and cool on a wire rack. Store the tea cakes in a cookie jar or other airtight container.

EXTRA TRACKS

Every cook has a few recipes that don't necessarily fit into a particular course or category. They might be pickles or a special spice rub or sauce. This chapter is my grandma's attic of hodgepodge recipes that I love and use often but that don't quite fit into a particular chapter of this book. That doesn't mean they are any less important, though, and you'll find me referring to them throughout the book.

MARY STRAUSS'S MOTHER'S CRANBERRY SAUCE

I learned this recipe from Mrs. Mary Strauss when I was a kidney dialysis technician caring for her husband, Leon, who later became the first supporter of Sweetie Pie's. I give a small jar of this cranberry sauce to everyone who comes to the employee Thanksgiving dinner we hold at the restaurant. It gives them a head start on Christmas dinner, as it's perfect served with a holiday turkey.

MAKES 8 (8-OUNCE) JARS

2 (12-ounce) bags fresh or
   frozen cranberries
4 cups sugar
½ cup water
Juice of 1 lemon
2 cups orange marmalade
1 (12-ounce) jar pineapple
   preserves
¼ cup raisins (optional)

1. Place the cranberries in a large saucepan and add the sugar, water, and lemon juice. Place over medium-low heat, bring to a simmer, and simmer until the cranberries become tender and start to break down, about 25 minutes.

2. Pour in the orange marmalade and pineapple preserves and stir well. Add the raisins, if using. Reduce the heat to low and cook until thickened like jelly, about 30 minutes.

3. Remove the cranberry sauce from the heat, cool completely, then pour into 8-ounce mason jars. Refrigerate.

MISS ROBBIE'S BETTER-THAN-VELVEETA® CHEESE SPREAD

Did you ever wonder why a lot of products in the supermarket are called "cheese food" or "cheese spread"? When I checked it out, I discovered that it's because there's usually no real cheese in them! Still, I'll be the first to tell you that there's nothing like Velveeta to make macaroni and cheese creamy. Since I didn't want to give that up but I like to know what's in my food, I decided to do what I do best and create my own. This is my own recipe for a Velveeta-type cheese—except you'll see there's plenty of real cheese in it! You can make this up and keep it in the fridge wrapped real tight. Use it the way you would any store-bought cheese product.

MAKES 2 (1-POUND) BLOCKS

1 packet powdered gelatin

2 tablespoons water

1 cup milk

¼ cup nonfat milk powder

2 teaspoons salt

¼ teaspoon ground turmeric

1 pound shredded sharp
   cheddar cheese

½ pound shredded Colby Jack
   cheese

1. In a small bowl, sprinkle the gelatin over the water and let it stand for 5 minutes or so.

2. In a medium saucepan, combine the milk, milk powder, salt, and turmeric and whisk well to dissolve the milk powder. Bring the mixture just up to a scald, but do not let it boil.

3. Put the cheeses in a food processor, add about a quarter of the hot milk mixture, and pulse for about 30 seconds. You'll see the cheese start to break down and melt.

4. Add the gelatin mixture and another quarter of the hot milk and pulse it again so it's well combined.

5. Add the rest of the milk in a steady stream through the hole in the top, pulsing until it's nice and smooth, scraping down the sides of the processor bowl with a rubber spatula if needed, 2 to 3 minutes.

6. Cut two 8 x 6-inch pieces of waxed or parchment paper and another two 6 x 14-inch pieces. Get two 4 x 6-inch loaf pans.

7. Line one loaf pan with a piece of the 8 x 6-inch waxed paper so the edges hang over the long sides. Then lay the 6 x 14-inch

piece in the pan the long way so the edges hang over the sides. Repeat with the other pan.

8. Pour the cheese mixture equally between the two pans. Hold each pan with two hands and give it a good tap on the table to take out any air bubbles.

9. Wrap up each pan with plastic wrap. Go around twice to make sure it stays moist.

10. Let the cheese set up overnight in the refrigerator. When you take it out, those overhanging pieces of waxed paper will let you lift out the cheese block easily. Peel away the waxed paper and store the cheese in a zip-top bag or wrapped up in plastic wrap. The Better-Than-Velveeta® spread will keep up to one month, wrapped well and refrigerated.

NO-SALT SEASONING MIX

Seasoning salt is another one of those flavor-enhancing ingredients that's great to have on hand to give dash to a variety of dishes. A lot of the brands on the shelf at the market have too much salt, and I know a lot of folks are trying to watch that part of their diets. That's why I'm giving you my personal at-home recipe that you can mix up and keep on hand for your dishes. Lots of flavor and none of the salt!

MAKES ABOUT ½ CUP

1 tablespoon sweet paprika

¼ teaspoon smoked paprika

1½ tablespoons ground
   turmeric

1 tablespoon onion powder

1 tablespoon garlic powder

¼ teaspoon ground black
   pepper

2 teaspoons sugar

½ teaspoon cornstarch

In a medium bowl, mix all the ingredients well. Store in a lidded jar or zip-top bag. Use as you would any seasoning salt.

OVER-THE-TOP HOMEMADE ONION SOUP MIX

When I was on the road or working full time and my kids were young, I had to take short-cuts to get a meal on the table. What with nine kids, my mom did too. It was handy to have packaged onion soup or some cheese around to give a dish extra flavor. But the more I cook the more I've come to know that homemade is always best. Believe it or not, it's just about as easy to make these things at home and keep them on hand as it is to get them at the store. It's cheaper in the long run too.

I use this mix to give flavor to my meatloaf, stuffed peppers, and any number of dishes you find in Sweetie Pie's Cookbook. It comes right after the salt and pepper in nearly everything I cook. Of course, you can always use the store mix, but I promise you, it won't be as good as mine.

MAKES 2 CUPS

¾ cup beef bouillon powder

¾ cup dried minced onion

½ cup onion powder

4 teaspoons parsley flakes

1 tablespoon ground turmeric

¼ teaspoon ground cumin

1 tablespoon celery salt

1 teaspoon salt

1 teaspoon ground black pepper

1½ tablespoons light brown sugar

1. Put all of the ingredients in a food processor or other grinder and pulse until it's mostly powder; you should still be able to see bits of the dried minced onion.

2. Store in an airtight jar or zip-top bag. Use about 3 tablespoons of the mix to equal one packet of commercial mix.

miss robbie says . . . back it up! Because I use so much of this mix, I like to double or triple the recipe and store it in tightly sealed jars. Small jars make a nice holiday gift; put one in a basket with Mary Strauss's Mother's Cranberry Sauce (page 178) and No-Salt Seasoning Mix (page 182).

BARBECUE SAUCE

You can always buy barbecue sauce that's to your taste—there are so many kinds on the market now—but this is the one I've come up with over the years, and it's what we use when we make our barbecued St. Louis spareribs at Sweetie Pie's.

MAKES 1½ QUARTS
(ENOUGH FOR 2 RACKS
OF RIBS)

2 cups tomato sauce or
   ketchup
1 cup Italian-style salad
   dressing
½ 5-ounce bottle Tabasco
   sauce
½ 10-ounce bottle steak sauce
½ 10-ounce bottle
   Worcestershire sauce
½ cup vegetable oil
1 cup sugar
¼ cup maple syrup
Salt and pepper

In a large bowl, combine all the ingredients and whisk well. Use on Sweetie Pie's Tender Oven-Baked St. Louis–Style BBQ Ribs (page 47) or on any barbecued meat dish.

ENCHILADA SAUCE

It's easy to make enchilada sauce, and you can go beyond tacos, tamales, or burritos with it. It can even serve as a simple sauce for grilled meat or as the basis for chili.

MAKES 3 CUPS

¼ cup extra virgin olive oil

2 cloves garlic, minced

1 small onion, minced

1 tablespoon all-purpose flour

2 cups canned crushed tomatoes

1 cup tomato sauce

1 teaspoon ground cumin

¼ teaspoon ground turmeric

1 teaspoon salt

¼ teaspoon chili powder

2 teaspoons dark brown sugar

1½ cups water

1. Heat the oil in a large saucepan over medium heat. Add the garlic and onion and cook, stirring, for 1 to 2 minutes, then add the flour. Cook, continuing to stir, for a couple minutes more, until the flour is a light brown color; don't let the flour get too brown.

2. Add the crushed tomatoes and tomato sauce, then stir in the cumin, turmeric, salt, chili powder, and brown sugar. Mix well, then add the water. Simmer for 10 to 12 minutes, then turn off the heat and let cool. The sauce will keep in the refrigerator in a well-sealed container for up to 1 week.

MISS ROBBIE'S RECIPE PLAYLISTS

menus

In this section, what I've done is put together a few of my favorite menus for entertaining and for family meals. Go on ahead and change up anything you like to make the menu your own.

HEAVEN'S DOOR SUNDAY BRUNCH

I named this brunch menu after my salmon croquettes, which I like to serve on buttermilk biscuits. They're so good that after one bite you'll feel like you died and went straight on up to knock on heaven's door.

Brunch is a good way to have folks over without all the trouble of a big party. It's casual and there's something for everyone with flavors sweet as well as salty. Now I don't know if they serve brunch in heaven, but this lineup is like a little bit of paradise on earth.

HOLE IN ONE (PAGE 2)

SALMON CROQUETTES (PAGE 12) ON BAKING POWDER BISCUITS (PAGE 127)

CHICKEN SALAD (PAGE 16) WITH WHOLE WHEAT CRACKERS

STUFFED PEPPERS (PAGE 67)

HOT HONEY WINGS (PAGE 24)

GARLICKY GREEN BEANS (PAGE 86)

CINNAMON ROLLS WITH CREAM CHEESE FROSTING (PAGE 130)

SUNDAY SUPPER MENU

When I was growing up, we always had roast beef (page 74) for Sunday supper. My mom was a housewife, and she could put in the time to get that kind of meal together. Today most folks are out and about on the weekend, catching up for the coming week, and that's why I like this menu that features economical and easy-to-prepare baked chicken as the star. After trying this menu out, you'll want to make Sunday supper a regular thing in your house if it isn't already.

BAKED CHICKEN AND RICE (PAGE 32)

MIXED GREENS (PAGE 87)

ROBERTA'S GRANDMOTHER'S YEAST ROLLS (PAGE 128)

CANDIED CARROT SOUFFLÉ (PAGE 99)

PINEAPPLE UPSIDE-DOWN CAKE (PAGE 168)

SUMMER BARBECUE MENU

Summer isn't summer without more than a few barbecues, and in the South barbecue is serious business. Deviled eggs and coleslaw are definitely going to be on the menu, and here in St. Louis, you have to have ribs. If you aren't a fan of ribs, this menu is just as good with Fried Chicken (page 35) or even burgers (page 64).

DEVILED EGGS (PAGE 11)

COLESLAW (PAGE 17)

SWEETIE PIE'S TENDER OVEN-BAKED ST. LOUIS–STYLE BBQ RIBS (PAGE 47)

THE BIG MO (PAGE 64)

ONIONY ROASTED CORN (PAGE 102)

POTATO SALAD (PAGE 14)

PEAR COBBLER (PAGE 184)

EASTER MENU

Ham is a must-have for a lot of families' Easter table, but my favorite part of this meal is the Crab Dip, which is a good way to start the meal off feeling special. If you don't like ham, Sunday Roast Beef (page 74) or Roast Turkey (page 37) are good substitutes, and so are either of my whole fish recipes (pages 28 to 29).

CRAB DIP (PAGE 8)

BAKED HAM (PAGE 44)

LIMA BEANS (PAGE 81)

POTATO PANCAKES (PAGE 113)

BREAD PUDDING (PAGE 172)

SCRIPTURE CAKE (PAGE 158)

HOT CROSS BUNS (PAGE 133)

CHRISTMAS MENU

Around here, Christmas dinner is pretty much the same as Thanksgiving, except I might add a ham or a roast beef into the bargain, along with some special dips like my Crab Dip (page 8) as appetizers before the meal. For this menu, I've created a roasted winter vegetable recipe to change it up a little. Of course, you should go on ahead and add or take away anything you like to make this holiday meal special for your family.

ROAST TURKEY (PAGE 37)

CORNBREAD DRESSING (PAGE 118)

MASHED TURNIPS (PAGE 116)

ROASTED WINTER VEGETABLES WITH MAPLE GLAZE (PAGE 104)

CANDIED YAMS (PAGE 114)

MASHED PUMPKIN WITH BUTTER AND CINNAMON (PAGE 100)

MARY STRAUSS'S MOTHER'S CRANBERRY SAUCE (PAGE 178)

BREAD PUDDING (PAGE 172)

DADDY'S SPECIAL-TREAT YELLOW CAKE WITH VANILLA SAUCE (PAGE 160)

EASY WEEKDAY DINNER MENU

After a long day at the restaurant, I sure don't feel like cooking. I know many of you can relate. Here is a good, simple menu that anyone could pull together, even after a long day, and still feel like you got a home cooked meal in.

TURKEY AND NOODLES (PAGE 42)
BELL PEPPER QUARTET (PAGE 91)
BREAD PUDDING (PAGE 172)

FRIED CHICKEN DINNER MENU

This menu is so much a part of who we are in the South it seems almost silly to write it down! You can have a fried chicken feast like this sitting around your dinner table or for a picnic or backyard party. Of course the Fried Green Tomatoes are a summer thing—but that doesn't mean you can't change that up with something different like succotash or okra and have this all year long.

FRIED CHICKEN (PAGE 35)
MASHED POTATOES (PAGE 112)
MAC AND CHEESE (PAGE 109)
COLLARD GREENS (PAGE 88)
FRIED GREEN TOMATOES (PAGE 92)
ICEBOX LEMON PIE (PAGE 146)

THANKSGIVING MENU

We always have Thanksgiving at the restaurant for our staff and their families, and this is the basic menu. Of course, folks bring all sorts of additions, and usually the buffet tables are just about collapsing under the weight of all the food. In addition to the cranberry sauce on the table, I give away little jars of homemade cranberry sauce (page 178) to everyone at the end of the meal for people to use with their Christmas dinner.

ROAST TURKEY (PAGE 37)

BAKED HAM (PAGE 44)

CHITTERLINGS (PAGE 52)

CORNBREAD DRESSING (PAGE 118)

MAC AND CHEESE (PAGE 109)

MASHED POTATOES (PAGE 112) OR POTATO SALAD (PAGE 14)

SOUL-STYLE SPAGHETTI WITH MEAT SAUCE (PAGE 110)

MIXED GREENS (PAGE 87)

CANDIED YAMS (PAGE 114)

BAKED BEANS (PAGE 82)

COLESLAW (PAGE 17)

MASHED PUMPKIN WITH BUTTER AND CINNAMON (PAGE 100)

MARY STRAUSS'S MOTHER'S CRANBERRY SAUCE (PAGE 178)

SKY-HIGH SWEET POTATO PIE (PAGE 144)

ROSALIE'S CHAMPION CHESS PIE (PAGE 138)

POUND CAKE (PAGE 157)

CARAMEL CAKE (PAGE 167)

HOLIDAY DESSERT PARTY MENU

Everyone loves the holidays, but no one loves the stress that goes along with them. Holidays are an especially busy time in the restaurant business, so you can imagine it's pretty hard to have folks over for a holiday party or get-together. I usually manage to get in a dessert party, though, because who doesn't like sweets? Folks come over, grab a treat and some coffee or tea, and stay awhile. There's almost no cleanup, especially if you use some of the pretty paperware that's available nowadays—and if you send your guests home with goodie bags of the leftovers!

MISS OZELA'S OLD-FASHIONED SOUTHERN TEA CAKES (PAGE 175)

CHOCOLATE CREAM PIE (PAGE 149)

POUND CAKE (PAGE 157) WITH SIX FLAVOR GLAZE (PAGE 166)

FRIED FRUIT PIES (PAGE 151)

PEANUT BRITTLE (PAGE 173)

ST. LOUIS GOOEY BUTTER CAKE (PAGE 164)

DO THE SWEETIE PIE

playlists/menus
from my own mixes

Now that you've gotten a taste of how I cook and feed my family and friends, you can put together your own favorite recipes from Sweetie Pie's Cookbook for special occasions and everyday events. Your family and friends will add in the background. I have only three pieces of advice for you: Make it your own, make it tasty, and make it sing!

YOUR OWN RECIPES/MENUS

ACKNOWLEDGMENTS

Cooking is something that you come by over many years of practice, so by the time you get set to put your recipes and thoughts down in a cookbook, the list of folks who have taught you their recipes and ways over the years gets to be mighty long.

Of course, the first person to thank is my mama, Ora Mae Montgomery, who was a great cook from a long line of great cooks and who taught me everything she knew.

If I didn't have the opportunity to tour with Tina and Ike Turner, I wouldn't have had the chance to become so creative with a hot plate and whatever ingredients were around—hard times make a cook really pull out all the stops. Cooking on the fly when I wasn't singing for my supper gave me strength and confidence, not just in the kitchen, but also in my life.

A special thank you goes to every one of my fellow band members, but most of all to Anna May—known to you as Tina Turner—for loving my cooking as much as she did.

Extra thanks to former Ikettes Venetta Fields, who loved my spaghetti, and Jessie Smith, who shared everything with me—hard times and good times.

I'll never forget how Jessie and I fed both of our families on a single chicken that time.

All of my friends who have shared their recipes so generously for this book—I'm grateful to you all as well as all of my family, who not only ate the good stuff but happily served as guinea pigs for my "flops" over the years too.

My son Tim deserves the most props for pushing me to do this book because he believed I could. All right, I'll say it for you Tim—you *did* tell me so, and you were right! Thank you.

I can never leave out Mr. Bussey, who keeps me on the straight and narrow (when I listen, that is).

Miss Robbie celebrating her seventy-second birthday.

My two most important thank-yous go first to all of the folks who come into Sweetie Pie's and who watch *Welcome to Sweetie Pie's* on the Oprah Winfrey Network. Your love and loyalty made me want to write this book and share my recipes and stories.

And second, but not ever last, I thank the good Lord, who has seen fit to give me chances and second chances and gifts that have made me rich in spirit every single day. My hope is to honor His faith in me by being a blessing to others just as so many have been a blessing to me.

INDEX

ABOUT THE AUTHOR

Miss Robbie Montgomery is the owner of Sweetie Pie's, the nationally acclaimed soul food restaurants she founded in her hometown of St. Louis, Missouri. Prior to running her own restaurants, Miss Robbie toured as a back-up singer for several musical artists including Ike and Tina Turner, the Supremes, Stevie Wonder, James Brown, Patti LaBelle, and others. Miss Robbie started cooking while she was traveling with these groups on the road, because finding welcoming restaurants could be challenging for African Americans in the segregated 1960s. After a collapsed lung prematurely ended Miss Robbie's singing career, she returned to St. Louis and began using her formidable cooking talent. In 2011, she opened her third restaurant location, Sweetie Pie's Upper Crust. Her restaurant reality show has been featured on the OWN Network.